BLACK&DECKER®

TRIM & FINISH CARPENTRY

Techniques & Tips from the Pros

Creative Publishing
international

MINNEAPOLIS, MINNESOTA
www.creativepub.com

Creative Publishing international

Copyright © 2010
Creative Publishing international, Inc.
400 First Avenue North, Suite 300
Minneapolis, Minnesota 55401
1-800-328-0590
www.creativepub.com

Printed in China

10 9 8 7 6 5 4 3

Library of Congress Cataloging-in-Publication Data

Trim & finish carpentry : techniques & tips from the pros.
   p. cm.
 At head of title: Black & Decker.
 Summary: "For the DIYer, this volume shows homeowners the tips
and techniques pros use to get beautiful precision when installing crown moldings, chair rails, paneling, and window and door
millwork. Includes live-action DVD"-- Provided by publisher.
 Includes index.
 ISBN-13: 978-1-58923-523-6 (soft cover)
 ISBN-10: 1-58923-523-1 (soft cover)
 1. Trim carpentry--Amateurs' manuals. 2. Finish carpentry--Ama-
teurs' manuals. I. Black & Decker Corporation (Towson, Md.) II. Title:
Trim and finish carpentry.

 TH5695.T695 2009
 694'.6--dc22

2010013578

Trim & Finish Carpentry
Created by: The Editors of Creative Publishing international, Inc. in cooperation with Black & Decker. Black & Decker® is a trademark of The
Black & Decker Corporation and is used under license.

President/CEO: Ken Fund

Home Improvement Group

Publisher: Bryan Trandem
Managing Editor: Tracy Stanley
Senior Editor: Mark Johanson

Creative Director: Michele Lanci-Altomare
Art Direction/Design: Jon Simpson, Brad Springer, James Kegley

Lead Photographer: Joel Schnell
Set Builder: James Parmeter
Production Managers: Laura Hokkanen, Linda Halls

Page Layout Artist: Christopher Fayers
Shop Help: Charles Boldt
Edition Editor: John Langan
Proofreader: Jean Cook, ImageSmythe

NOTICE TO READERS

For safety, use caution, care, and good judgment when following the procedures described in this book. The Publisher and Black & Decker cannot assume responsibility for any damage to property or injury to persons as a result of misuse of the information provided.

The techniques shown in this book are general techniques for various applications. In some instances, additional techniques not shown in this book may be required. Always follow manufacturers' instructions included with products, since deviating from the directions may void warranties. The projects in this book vary widely as to skill levels required: some may not be appropriate for all do-it-yourselfers, and some may require professional help.

Consult your local Building Department for information on building permits, codes and other laws as they apply to your project.

Contents

Trim & Finish Carpentry

Introduction

Trim moldings are installed primarily to decorate our houses by adding rich wood tones and creating ornamental effects that often feature light and shadow. Moldings do perform minor structural jobs, too, mainly to conceal gaps between walls, floor, and ceilings, and around doors and windows.

Decorative trim has a long history. Ancient Greeks used molding in their buildings to divide surfaces into smaller parts to create visual interest, generally basing their profiles on the ellipse, parabola, or hyperbola. Romans simplified the moldings of the Greeks, basing their profiles instead on the circle. These two styles of molding evolved into eight classical shapes of molding, derived from a combination of complex moldings that have irregular curvatures and simple moldings formed from a continuous curve, such as the arc of a circle.

Traditional trim molding has details and features that identify it as belonging to a particular architectural style. The most popular styles for millwork are Victorian, Federal, Arts & Crafts, Neoclassical, and modern. Some of these profiles have served as the building blocks of interior ornament for centuries. It should be noted that a large portion of the floor space given over to moldings at any building center these days is consumed by ranch molding—a "style" of trim that is so plain it has no real style classification. Ranch moldings are cheap and easy to install and thus have some value as a building material. But if your intent is to use trim as a significant decorative element in your home, you should investigate some of the more interesting profiles (see pages 26 to 31).

Until the middle of the 1800s, most molding in America was made on the building site by carpenters who used hand planes, chisels, and gouges. Wide pieces of trim, such as crown molding, were made in woodworking shops where large planes were pulled by apprentices under the guidance of master artisans. Depending on the size and style of a building, molding could be used to ornament almost all the interior architectural elements.

By the late 1850s, planing machines had been developed to produce molding on a large scale, at a much lower cost than custom handmade molding. This made elaborate and sophisticated ornamentation available to all who wanted it in their homes. In today's market it would not be cost effective for carpenters to create molding profiles from lumber. Today, mass-production brings a whole range of molding possibilities to any home builder or remodeler, from re-creations of built-up cornices to replications of hand-carved plaster moldings made from a mold and cast polyurethane. Creative trim carpenters have learned to combine stock moldings to create a nearly infinite variety of complex profiles.

Before beginning your trim project, do plenty of planning and get to know your tools. Safety is paramount when working with any power tools. Make sure you use the correct tools for the project and that the tools are well maintained. Also use proper techniques and safety practices: Carelessness is not only dangerous; it can lead to inaccurate measurements, poor cuts, and loss of productivity.

Victorian Trim Style

Victorian style began in the mid-nineteenth century and lasted approximately sixty years. Trimwork of this style is generally very ornate with large elaborate casings that emphasize curves and decoration rather than material. Moldings were built by stacking layers multiple times, rather than using a single piece.

Victorian style is generally seen in houses with higher ceilings. Due to the sheer size and nature of these moldings, they may tend to crowd a standard 8-ft.-tall room, especially if all types of trim elements are included from the floor up. However, the term "Victorian" encompasses many different variations and can be successfully installed in smaller homes by sizing down the scale of the trimwork.

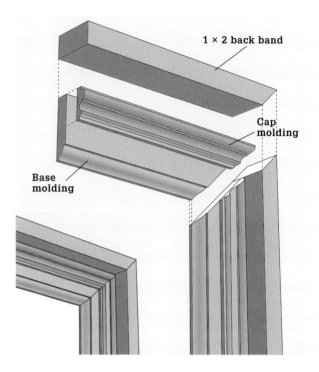

This Victorian door casing is not made up of casing at all, but actually a combination of baseboard and cap molding with 1 × 2 as a back band. The overall width of the casing is 4", creating a strong statement when compared to a single-piece stock molding.

Victorian frame and panel walls were often so elaborate that they were constructed outside the home and brought in to be installed.

Baseboards were commonly 7" tall or greater, with plinth blocks at door openings rather than a straight casing to the floor.

Victorian style cornice moldings were often very large and elaborate. Made up of multiple pieces of material, the decoration can sometimes be seen as out of proportion with current construction standards.

Arts & Crafts Trim Style

Arts & Crafts style originated near the turn of the twentieth century. Trim components of this style generally emphasize wood grain, function, and simplicity in design. Typical Arts & Crafts furnishings and trim are made from quartersawn white oak, but painted trim work is a less expensive alternative that still maintains the style.

There are many variations of Arts & Crafts style. The projects provided in this book illustrate only a few common trim techniques. Research the movement if you like the idea of wider, straight-line casings, but don't see exactly what you want. The installation techniques are the same, with variations in joinery and style elements.

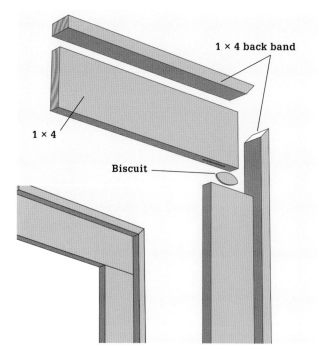

Use biscuits to join butted joints of an Arts & Crafts window or door treatment. Mitered corner molding wraps around the perimeter of the solid stock, to add depth to the casing.

Decorative elements from these Arts & Crafts cabinets are repeated in the window frame and throughout the room to an impressive visual effect.

White oak is the preferred Arts & Crafts wood type. The window apron above is from quartersawn white oak, the preferred cut. The wainscot panels are plainsawn white oak veneer plywood.

Arts & Crafts plate rail doubles as wainscot cap, which is usually higher than wainscot in other decorating vernaculars. In a typical Arts & Crafts installation, the wainscot is between 48" and 54" high. Corbels located above frame-and-panel stiles are a common motif.

Fancy Arts & Crafts embellishments, like the newel post (above) and the wraparound window header (left), still feature relatively plain wood treatments with a very linear appearance.

Neoclassical Trim Style

The term "Neoclassical" refers to any style derived from classic Roman or Greek architecture. Specific Neoclassical styles include Federal and Georgian styles. Traditional Greek buildings had structural components such as columns and pedestals, which, in modern time, have been replaced with interior trim elements such as door casings and baseboard. An example of a Neoclassical door trim would be a fluted casing with plinth blocks at the floor. This style is a direct, but flatter version, of classic Greek architecture.

Neoclassical style is also represented in many of the buildings of the U.S. Federal Government. Many national monuments have Neoclassical elements in their window and door treatments as well as the obvious exterior trim components such as columns.

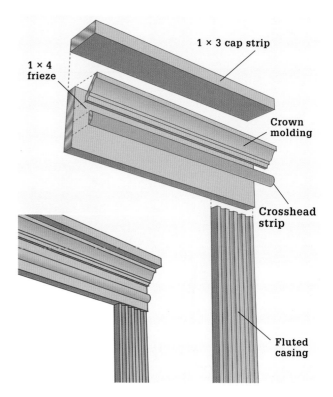

This illustrated Neoclassical fluted casing (right) is capped off with a 4-piece decorative head including: half-round crosshead strip, 1 × 4 frieze board, crown molding, and 1 × 3 cap strip.

Neoclassical is a very broad trim category that includes many styles and interpretations. Basically, it boils down to "Formal and Fancy."

In this Neoclassical doorway, decorative "keystones" highlight the archway over the door and are repeated in the cornice molding as well.

Not all Neoclassical trim is extremely ornate. The clean lines of this door casing and plinth blocks are crisp and graceful, an effect that is enhanced by the white painted finish.

Neoclassical moldings often are very ornate, like this Federal-style exterior door head molding.

Dentil moldings are also common in crown moldings, mantels, and frieze boards.

Modern Trim Style

Modern style is relatively plain, downplaying decorative carving or complex profiles. Where Victorian trim pieces are elaborate multiple-piece moldings high on decoration, modern trim can be as basic as plywood cut to a uniform width with clean lines and butted joints. Hardware on modern cabinetry, doors, and windows is generally sleek, with chrome or black oxide coating. Six-panel doors are replaced with slab doors and industrial materials are incorporated into the design whenever possible, including revealing the internal systems of a home such as heating ducts and electrical lines.

Moreso than the styles of the past, modern style represents a complete change in how we view trim and architecture. Traditional ideas about what materials should be used and where and how they are installed are challenged. The focus of modern style is function, never purely decoration.

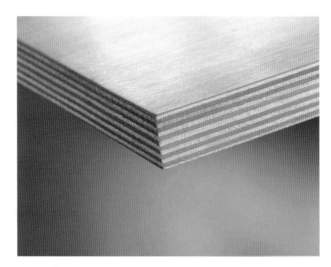

Birch plywood, commonly known as Baltic Birch, is frequently used to make Modern style trim. The plywood is ripped to strips of desired width and installed with an exposed plywood edge.

Modern trim isn't defined by any specific profiles or shapes—it simply is trim that has a clean, simple, and open appearance that's unlike the fanciness of the tradional styles.

Clean lines and hard shadows are the hallmarks of modern trim. White semi-gloss paint is the finish of choice.

Plain Colonial or ranch casings are mitered at the header of the door in the typical Modern home. Matching base moldings are butted against the door casings without a plinth block.

Glass block is a Modern-style material that allows light into a room without sacrificing safety. The window trim shown is made of ceramic tile rather than wood.

Dining Room Trim

36 lin. ft. - 3" door Casing - oak.
18 lin. ft. - 2 ¼" window Casing - oak
6 - 3×3" Plinth blocks
50 lin. ft. - 4" base - oak
50 lin. ft. - ¾" cap - oak
50 lin. ft. - ¾" shoe - oak

Preparing for a Trim Project

Like other types of home improvement work, successful trim carpentry requires a good deal of careful preparation. However, where preparation for installing flooring or painting walls requires time with brushes and levelers and primers and such, preparing for trim installation is mostly a matter of thinking and making good choices. After all, the point of trim is often to conceal problems that resulted from inadequate preparation or poor execution.

The fundamental questions you need to answer during the preparation process are "What should I install?" and "How should I attach it?" The easy part of trim selection is determining the location (at the ceiling, along the floor, next to the window…). Then, you need to choose a trim profile and material. Finally, you'll have to specify a finish. Each step of this process requires some thought and some knowledge of the options.

Choosing a method of attachment is usually rather obvious. In almost all cases, pneumatic nails are the best choice. But not all walls will accept nails, and some heavier trim material may require the holding strength of screws, while other lighter ones should be attached with adhesives only. There is a lot to think about. But once you've answered the basic questions, devising a plan of attack is relatively simple.

This section shows:

- Choosing a style
- Tools & Materials
- Molding profiles
- Glues & Adhesives
- Screws & Nails
- Abrasives
- Wood Fillers
- Jobsite Preparation
- Estimating Material
- Planning a Deadline
- Planning a Trim Layout
- Removing Old Trim

Choosing a style

When you begin to design your new trim project, you will want to make choices about the style and the types of moldings that are most appropriate for your home. Balance and scale, existing furnishings, and the applied finish will all change the effect your project has on the room as well as the overall house.

Choosing a specific style for your trim project can be as difficult as the actual installation. Architectural styles evoke different feelings from each individual. To help you choose a style, start with the feeling that you are trying to achieve in the room. The simplistic nature of Arts & Crafts may be relaxing to you, or maybe you find it boorish and unappealing. Neoclassical style may create a formal appearance for a dining room or den. It is possible that maintaining the existing style of your home is important to you. Or perhaps you would prefer to change the style in an individual room to make it more relaxed than the rest of your home. Whatever the case is, keep in mind there are no rules written in stone that state what you can and cannot do.

When adding trim, it generally is best to stay within the same period or style as already exists in your house. Mixing periods of trim, when not handled thoughtfully, can be awkward and confusing to the eye.

The style of your house should inform your trim selection decisions. Try to match or complement existing trim, both interior and exterior.

Balance & Scale

Scale can be defined as the size of a particular object in relation to its surroundings. When considering a trim style, scale is very important because moldings that are too large or small might not have an impact on a room the way you had planned.

Moldings that are well balanced create a sense of comfort and stability in a room and are well proportioned to each other—that is, they are scaled proportionally. For example, if you originally wanted to install very tall base molding, the crown or cornice treatment should be similar in scale or the room may be thrown out of balance.

The Ancient Greeks used a scale of proportion that mimics that of a column. The general rule of thumb for a room with an 8 ft. ceiling is that the base should be a minimum of 5" wide, the chair rail a minimum of 3" wide (set at a height between 32 and 36" up from the floor), and the crown a minimum of 5" wide. The wall represents the column shaft, the base molding represents and the base, and the crown represents the capital.

When choosing trim elements for your project, keep in mind the existing moldings of the room so that the new trim will have the effect you desire. It is a good idea to maintain balance and scale.

While our eye, in general, does not like surprises when it comes to scale, it is possible to create effective illusions by violating the normal rules of proportional scale. For example, by trimming a small room with an elaborate built-up crown you can make the room appear taller. But use caution—if not handled gracefully the trick can backfire and simply make your room look small and cluttered.

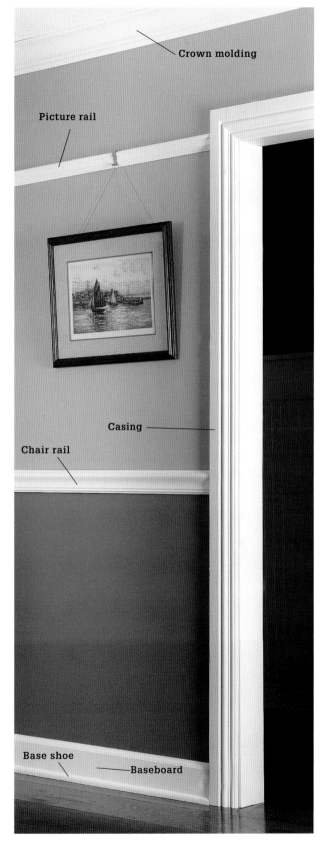

Scale can be used to your advantage—with an elaborate, built-up crown detail, this standard-height room looks like it has a taller ceiling than it actually does.

The style of the trim in this room is well balanced. The individual elements are similar in color and molding profile and do not overpower each other with strong differences in size.

Tools & Materials

Installing finish trim and casings is a challenging job that requires patience, attention to detail, and the right tool for each task. Without these requirements, the result will suffer. Start off right by using high-quality tools. Be sure to read and follow all safety instructions and become familiar with the tool and its operation prior to using it for your project. Good tools last longer and are generally more accurate than cheaper versions.

Many people buy tools only as they are needed to avoid purchases they will not use. This rationale should only apply to power tools and higher-priced specialty items. A high-quality basic tool set is important for every do-it-yourselfer to have on hand and ready when you need to use it. Doing so avoids improper tool usage and makes your job easier, with improved results.

necessary layout tools for basic trim jobs. Purchase the highest-quality layout tools you can afford. They are crucial for accurate measuring and marking of trim and help you avoid costly mistakes with expensive stock.

LAYOUT TOOLS

Layout tools help you measure, mark, and cut materials and surfaces with accuracy. Many layout tools are inexpensive and simply provide a means of measuring for level, square, and plumb lines. However, recent technologies have incorporated lasers into levels, stud finders, and tape measures, making them more accurate than ever before, at a slightly higher price. Although these new tools are handy in specific applications, their higher price is not always warranted and the average do-it-yourselfer can produce quality results without them.

Hand Tools

The hand tools you will need for most finish carpentry jobs can be broken down into two types: layout tools and construction tools. It is common for most people to own construction tools, but lack

- **A tape measure** A good quality tape with a thicker, reinforced tape will allow you to take longer measurements—up to 11 ft. without the tape buckling. The thicker tapes are also more durable. The constant extending and reeling in of the tape will put strain on the end, causing thinner tapes to rip and expose sharp edges.
- **A framing square**, also known as a carpenter's

Tape measure

Levels

Combination square

square, is commonly used to mark sheet goods and check recently installed pieces for position. Framing squares are also used as an initial check for wall squareness and plumb in relation to a floor or ceiling.

- **Chalk lines** are used to make temporary straight lines anywhere they are needed. The case of a chalk line, or the "box," is tear shaped so the tool doubles as a plumb bob. Use a chalk line to mark sheet goods for cutting or to establish a level line in a room. Keep in mind that chalk can be difficult to remove from porous surfaces.

- **A stud finder** is used to locate the framing members in a wall or ceiling. Higher-priced versions also find plumbing, electrical, or other mechanicals in the wall. Although a stud finder is not completely necessary, it is convenient when installing a larger job.

- **Levels** are available in a variety of lengths and price ranges. The longer and more accurate the level, the higher the price. The two most commonly used sizes are 2-ft. and 4-ft. lengths. The 2-ft. levels are handy for tighter spaces, while the 4-ft. variety serves as a better all-purpose level. Laser levels are handy for creating a level line around the perimeter of a room or for level lines along longer lengths. They provide a wide range of line or spot placement, depending on the model.

- **A T-bevel** is a specialized tool for finding and transferring precise angles. T-bevels are generally used in conjunction with a power miter saw to gauge angled miters of nonsquare corners. This tool is especially handy in older homes where the concepts of square, plumb, and level do not necessarily apply.

- **A profile gauge** uses a series of pins to recreate the profile of any object so that you may transfer it to a work piece. Profile gauges are especially useful when dealing with irregular obstructions.

- **A combination square** is a multifunction square that provides an easy reference for 45- and 90-degree angles, as well as marking reveal lines or a constant specific distance from the edge of a work piece.

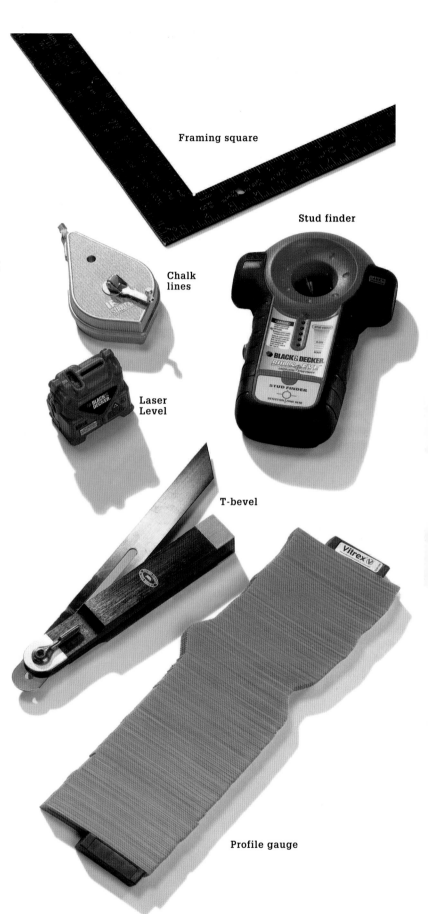

Framing square

Stud finder

Chalk lines

Laser Level

T-bevel

Profile gauge

CONSTRUCTION TOOLS

- **A good quality hammer** is a must for every trim carpentry project. A 16-oz. curved claw hammer, otherwise known as a finish hammer, is a good all-purpose choice.
- **Utility knives** are available in fixed, retracting, and retractable blades. This tool is used for a wide variety of cutting tasks from pencil sharpening to back-beveling miter joints. Always have additional blades readily available.
- **A set of chisels** is necessary for installing door hardware as well as notching trim around obstacles and final fitting of difficult pieces.
- **Block planes** are used to fit doors into openings and remove fine amounts of material from trim. A finely tuned block plane can even be used to clean up a sloppy miter joint.
- **A coping saw** has a thin, flexible blade designed to cut curves and is essential for making professional trim joints on inside corners. Coping saw blades should be fine toothed, between 16 and 24 teeth per inch for most hardwoods, and set to cut on the pull stroke of the saw to offer you more blade control.
- **A sharp handsaw** is convenient for quick cut-offs and in some instances where power saws are difficult to control. Purchase a cross-cut saw for general-purpose cutting.
- **Protective wear**, including safety glasses and ear protection, is required any time you are working with tools. Dust masks are necessary when sanding.
- **Pry bars** come in a variety of sizes and shapes. A quality forged high-carbon steel flat bar is the most common choice for trim projects. Wrecking bars make lighter work of trim and door removal due to their added weight.
- **Side cutters and end nippers** are useful for cutting off and pulling out bent nails. The added handle length and curved head of end nippers makes them ideal for larger casing nails. Pneumatic brad nails and smaller pins will pull out easier with side cutters. Purchase a nail set for countersinking nail heads. Three-piece sets are available for different nail sizes.
- **A rasp and a metal file set** are important for fitting coped joints precisely. The variety of shapes, sizes, and mills allows faster rougher removal of material or smoother slower removal, depending on the file.
- **Use a putty knife** to fill nail holes with putty and for light scraping tasks.

Pry bars

Protective wear

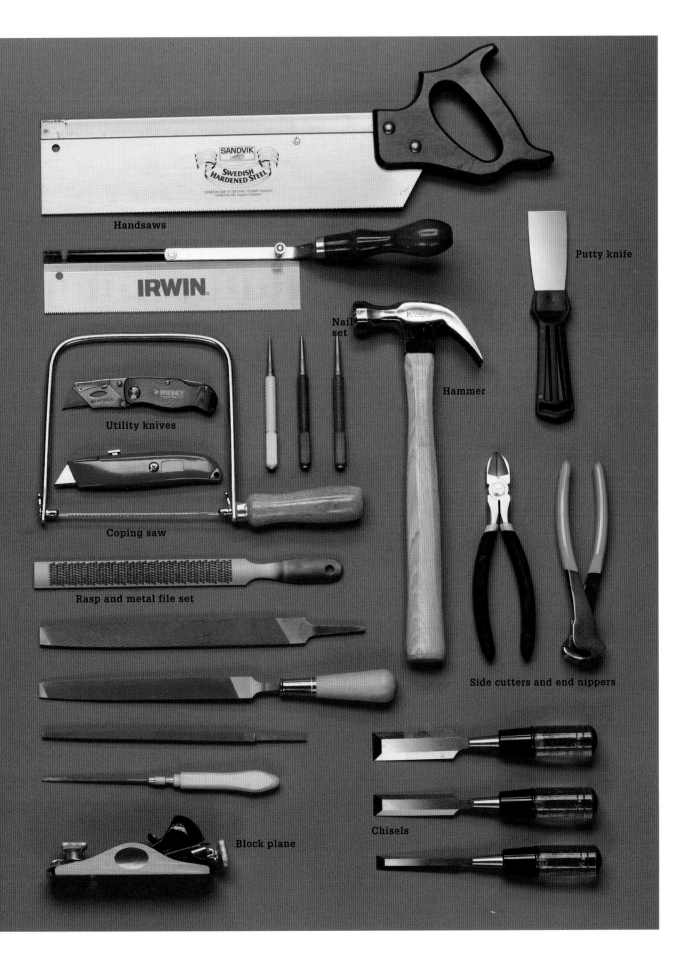

Handsaws

Putty knife

Nail set

Hammer

Utility knives

Coping saw

Rasp and metal file set

Side cutters and end nippers

Chisels

Block plane

Power Tools

Despite the higher price as compared to hand tools, power tools are a great value. They allow you to do work more quickly and accurately than with hand tools and make repetitive tasks like sanding, drilling, and sawing more enjoyable. Basic trim jobs do not require every power tool shown here, but some tools, such as a power miter box, are crucial for professional results. Purchase power tools on an as-needed basis, keeping in mind that while the cheapest tool is not always your best option, the most expensive and powerful is probably not necessary, either. Cheaper tools generally sacrifice precision, while the most expensive tools are made for people who use them every day, not just for occasional use. Power tools that are midrange in price are a good choice for the do-it-yourselfer.

- **A cordless drill** is one of the handiest tools available. Although drills are not normally used to install trim, they make quick work of installing wood backing for wainscoting and other trim features. Occasionally, trim head screws are used rather than nails to install trim. This situation is most common with steel-stud walls and necessitates a drill.
- **A circular saw** is ideal for straight cuts in plywood and quick cut-offs of solid material. Purchase a plywood blade to make smooth cuts in plywood and a general-purpose blade for other cuts.
- **A jigsaw** is the perfect tool for cutting curves, or notching out trim around obstructions. Jigsaw blades come in an array of designs for different

Compound power miter saw

Circular saw

Jigsaw

Reciprocating saw

Cordless drill/driver

styles of cuts and different types and thicknesses of materials. Always use the right type of blade and do not force the saw during the cut or it may bend or break.

- **A biscuit joiner** is a specialty tool used to make strong joints between two square pieces of stock.
- **A reciprocating saw** is used for removal and tear-down applications for trim projects. This tool is especially handy to remove door jambs.
- **A power miter saw**, or chop saw, will yield professional trim results. Most have a 10" or 12" diameter blade. A compound power miter saw has a head that pivots to cut bevels and miters at the same time. Sliding miter saws have more cutting capacity but are less portable. A fine-tooth carbide-tipped blade is best for trim projects.
- **A belt sander** is not essential but is a handy tool for quick removal of material.

- **Random-orbit sanders** are a good choice for smoothing flat areas, such as plywood, quickly. Random-orbit sanders leave no circular markings, like a disc sander, and can sand in any direction regardless of wood grain.
- **Finish sanders** are available in a variety of sizes and shapes for different light sanding applications.
- **A power planer** is used to trim doors to fit openings and flatten or straighten out materials. Power planes are faster to use than manual hand planes, but results are more difficult to control.
- **A tablesaw** is the best tool for ripping stock to width, and larger models can be fitted with a molding head for cutting profiles.
- **A router** (plunge router is shown here) has many uses in trim carpentry, especially for cutting edge profiles to make your own custom wood trim.

Router

Random-orbit sander

Biscuit, or plate, joiner

Power planer

Finish, or detail, sander

Belt sander

Tablesaw

Pneumatic Tools

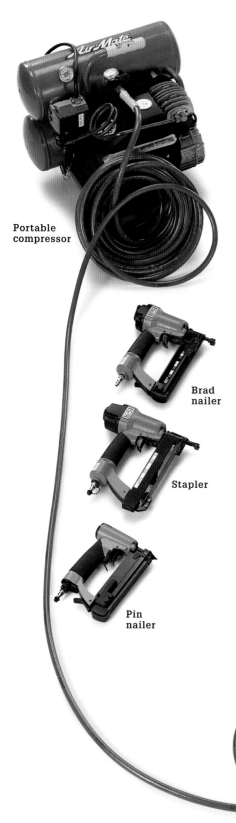

Portable compressor

Brad nailer

Stapler

Pin nailer

Angled finish nailer

Along with a good power miter saw, pneumatic tools are the key to timely, professional trim results. Pneumatic tools save time and energy over traditional hammer-and-nail installation. Not only do they drive fasteners quickly, but they countersink at the same time, avoiding multiple strikes to the trim, which could throw joints out of alignment. Predrilled holes are not necessary with pneumatic tools. Splitting occurs infrequently if the work piece is held firmly in place and the nails are positioned at least 1" from trim ends. Nail guns also allow you to concentrate on the placement of the work piece with one hand and fasten it with the other. You needn't fumble around with single fasteners because they are already loaded in the gun.

Cost of pneumatic tools, compressors, and fasteners has decreased over the years, making them not only the professional's choice, but a great option for the do-it-yourselfer as well. Pneumatic kits are available at home centers with two different guns and a compressor at a value price. For smaller trim jobs, consider renting pneumatics.

Portable compressors are available in different styles, including pancake and tumbler styles. Any compressor with air pressure of 90 psi or greater will work for a finish gun or brad nailer. Consider options like tank size, weight of the unit, and noise levels while the compressor is running. Talk to a home center specialist about what your specific compressor needs are and keep in mind any future pneumatic tools you might want.

The two basic pneumatic tools used in trim carpentry are a finish nailer, and a brad nailer. A finish nailer drives 15-gauge nails ranging from 1" to 2½". These nails work for a variety of moldings, door and window trim, and general-purpose fastening. Angled finish nailers are easier to maneuver in tight corners than straight guns, but either option will work. Brad nailers drive smaller 18-gauge fasteners ranging in length from ½" to 2". Some brad nailers' maximum length is 1¼". Because the fasteners are smaller, it is no surprise that the gun is lighter and smaller than a finish gun. Brad nailers are used to attach thinner stock, with less tendency of splitting the trim. Headless pinners drive fasteners similar to brad nailers without the head. These nails have less holding power, but are normally used to hold small moldings in place until the glue dries. Be sure to load headless pins with the points down, taking note of the label on the magazine. The ⅜" crown staplers are used to attach backing to trim pieces and in situations where maximum holding power is needed, but the fastener head will not be visible. Because staples have two legs and a crown that connects them, their holding power is excellent. However, the hole left by the staple's crown is large and can be difficult to fill.

▌Pneumatic Fasteners

The 15-gauge finish nails and angled finish nails range in length up to 2½". The angled variety are exactly the same as the straight nails, but come in angled clips. These nails are also available galvanized for exterior applications. Use finish nails to attach larger moldings and trim casings. Drive fasteners at regular intervals along the moldings and keep the position of the nails at least 1" from the molding ends. Fastener length is dependent upon the size of molding installed and what the backing is. Typical stock moldings are approximately ¾" thick. The fastener must pass through the molding and wallboard and into the stud behind. Generally, half the fastener should be embedded in the backing or stud, so in standard trim applications, 2" fasteners should suffice. 18-gauge brad nails range in length up to 2" for some guns and leave smaller holes to fill than finish guns. Brad nails are commonly used for thinner casings that are nailed directly to a solid backer. A specific example of this is along the inner edge of a door or window casing. The outer edge of the trim is nailed with a finish gun through the wallboard, while the inside edge rests against the door jamb, so it can be fastened with a brad nailer. Headless pins leave almost no nail hole to fill but are limited in length to 1". Their holding power is greatly diminished due to the lack of head, but they are generally used in conjunction with wood glue. Use ⅜" crown staples only when the fastener head will not be visible.

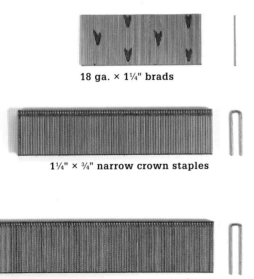

Cordless nailers offer the advantages of pneumatic nailers but without the trailing hose and the compressor. A battery-operated model, such as the 12-volt, 18-gauge brad nailer, is good for small jobs. Heavy-duty models powered by fuel cells can handle larger jobs but cost quite a bit more.

18 ga. × 1¼" brads

1¼" × ¾" narrow crown staples

⅜" × 1" narrow crown staples

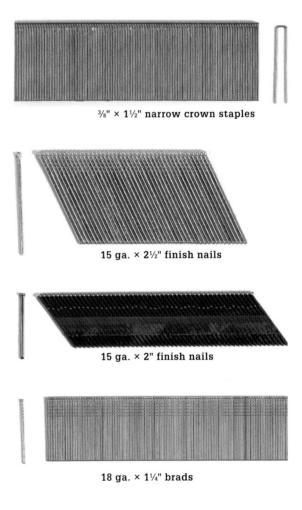

⅜" × 1½" narrow crown staples

15 ga. × 2½" finish nails

15 ga. × 2" finish nails

18 ga. × 1¼" brads

18 ga. × ⅝" brads

Molding Profiles

Trim moldings in stock profiles are available off the shelf at most home centers. Most molding manufacturers assign codes such as "WM166," or "HWM127" to every profile and size. However, you will find that the codes are not applied uniformly, making them virtually worthless if you're trying to track down specific molding profiles. The best way to order molding is to obtain a catalog from your molding supplier and use its labeling conventions.

There are a few conventions that are fairly consistently applied. In general, moldings labeled with a code starting with "WM" are paint-grade or softwood moldings. "HWM" designates the trim piece as a hardwood molding. If you like the style of a softwood molding, but would prefer to buy the piece in a hardwood species, ask for the equivalent in hardwood from the lumber yard sales associate.

Even though moldings are commonly found under categories such as "baseboard" or "cove," these categories relate to the style of the trim piece, not necessarily where it should be used. In fact, even among seasoned trim carpenters you'll frequently encounter arguments over which type a particular size or profile belongs to. The similarities are especially apparent when comparing base molding to case molding, as the following photos will confirm.

Mini-Glossary of Molding Shapes & Profiles ▶

Bead—A rounded profile

Chamfer—A 45° beveled edge profile

Dentil—A series of rectangular blocks spaced close together to form a border pattern

Flute—A shallow groove with a round profile, usually running longitudinally on the workpiece in groups of at least three

Frieze—Horizontal banding on the wall at the wall-ceiling joint

Ogee—An S-shape or reverse curve profile

Rosette—A square block with concentric circular carving, usually placed at the intersection of head and side casing

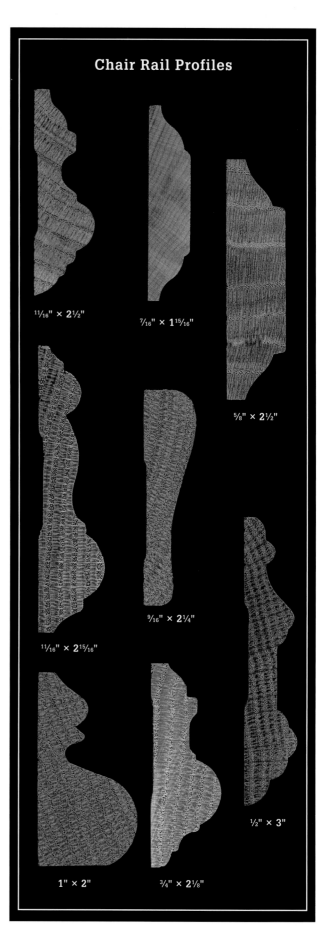

Chair Rail Profiles

11/16" × 2½"

7/16" × 1¹⁵/₁₆"

5/8" × 2½"

11/16" × 2¹⁵/₁₆"

9/16" × 2¼"

½" × 3"

1" × 2"

¾" × 2⅛"

Case Molding Profiles

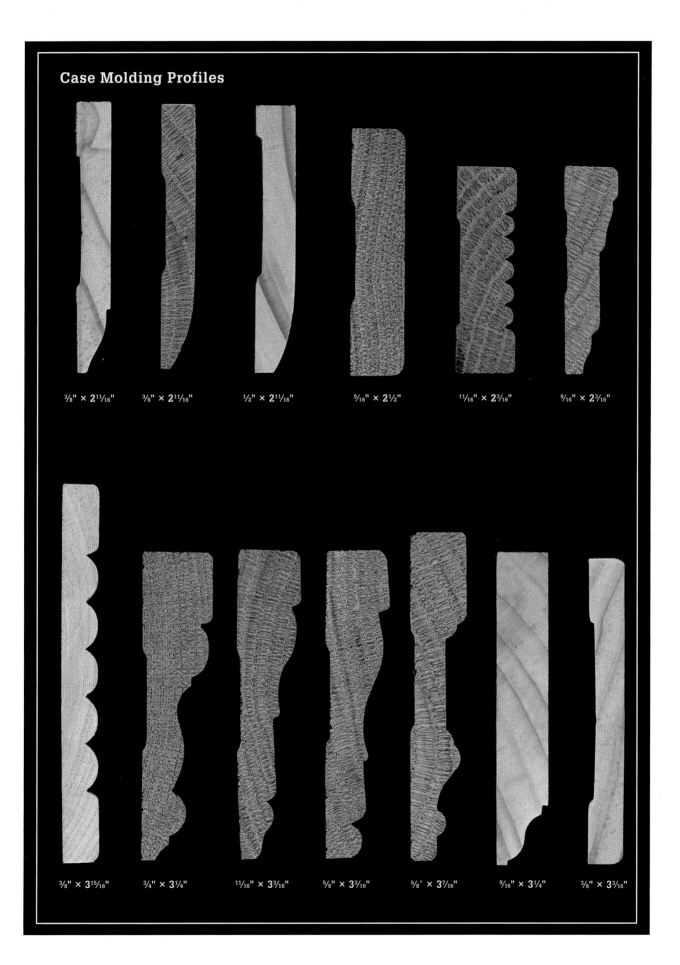

3/8" × 2¹¹⁄₁₆"   3/8" × 2¹¹⁄₁₆"   ½" × 2¹¹⁄₁₆"   9⁄₁₆" × 2½"   ¹¹⁄₁₆" × 2³⁄₁₆"   9⁄₁₆" × 2³⁄₁₆"

3/8" × 3¹⁵⁄₁₆"   ¾" × 3¼"   ¹¹⁄₁₆" × 3³⁄₁₆"   5/8" × 3³⁄₁₆"   5/8" × 3⁷⁄₁₆"   9⁄₁₆" × 3¼"   3/8" × 3³⁄₁₆"

Base Molding Profiles

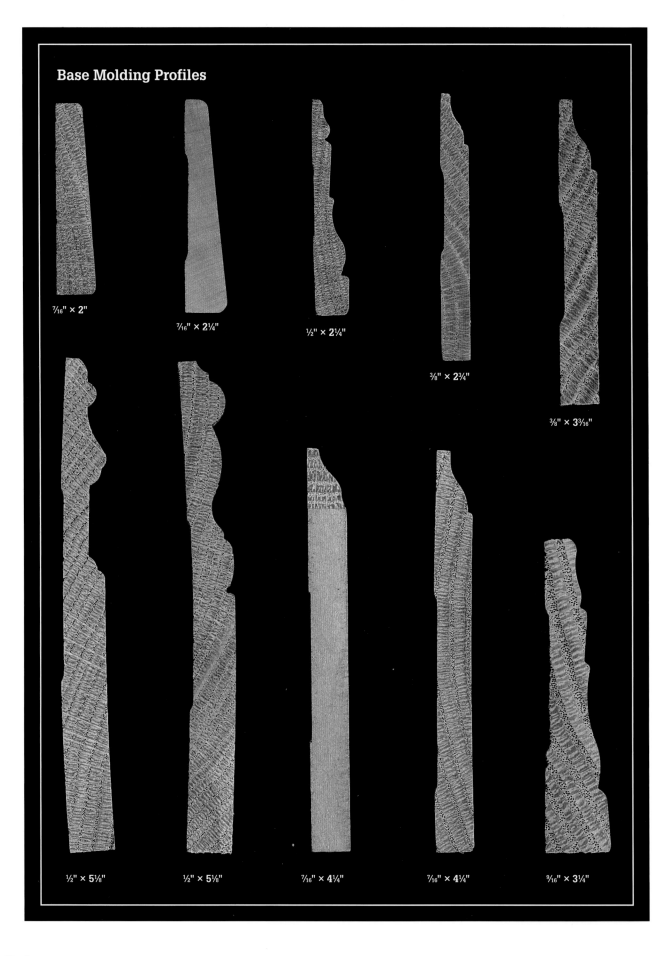

⁷⁄₁₆" × 2"

⁷⁄₁₆" × 2¼"

½" × 2¼"

⅜" × 2¾"

⅜" × 3³⁄₁₆"

½" × 5⅛"

½" × 5⅛"

⁷⁄₁₆" × 4¼"

⁷⁄₁₆" × 4¼"

⁹⁄₁₆" × 3¼"

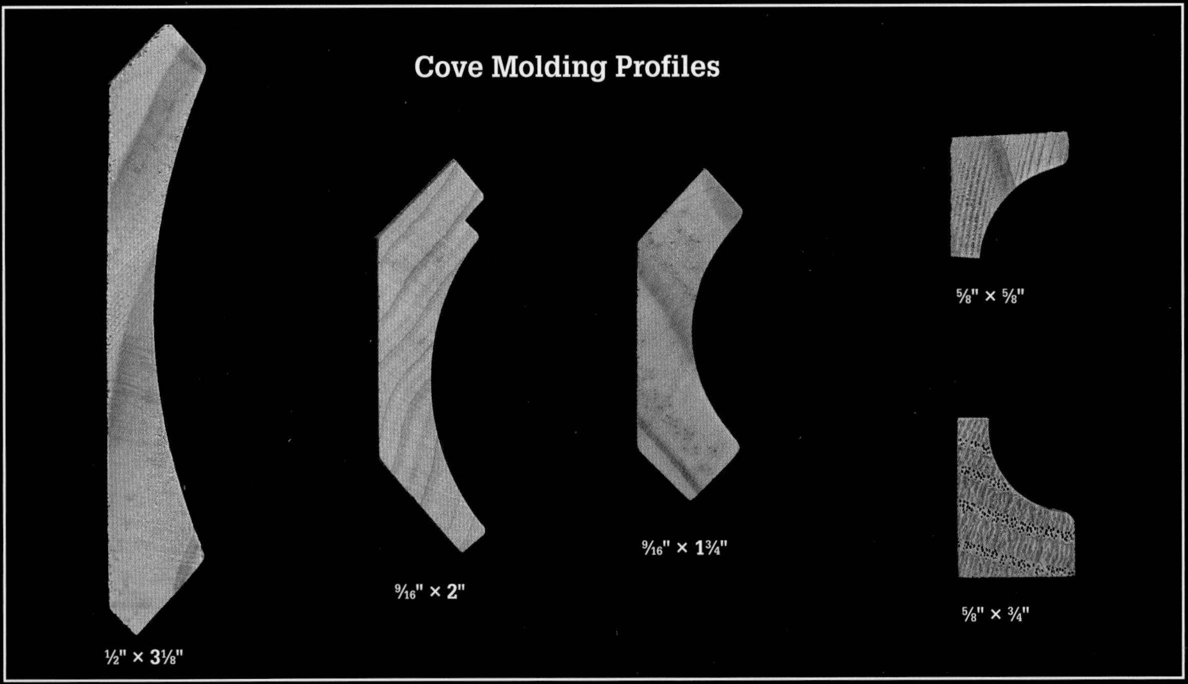
Cove Molding Profiles
½" × 3⅛"
9/16" × 2"
9/16" × 1¾"
⅝" × ⅝"
⅝" × ¾"

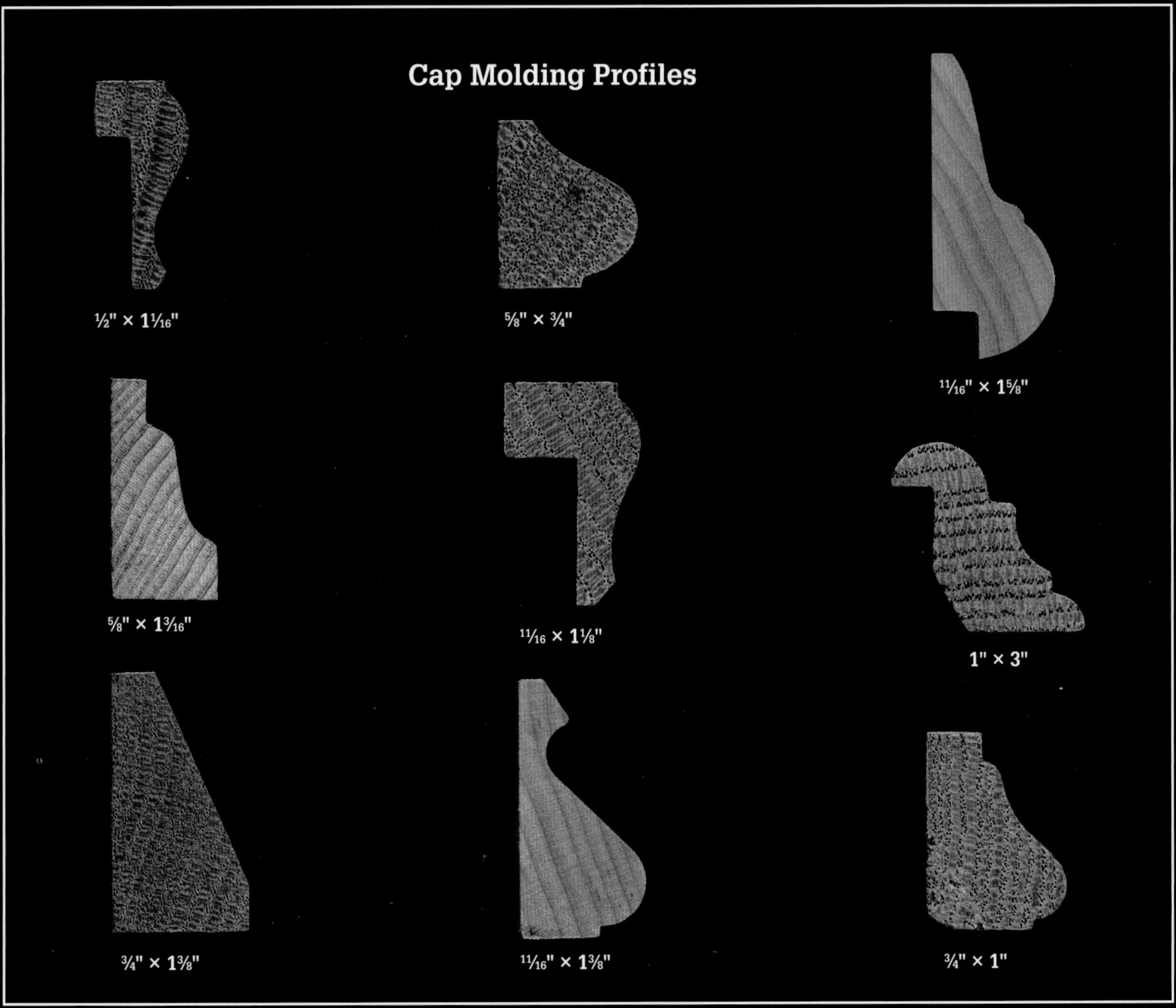
Cap Molding Profiles
½" × 1 1/16"
⅝" × ¾"
11/16" × 1⅝"
⅝" × 1 3/16"
11/16 × 1⅛"
1" × 3"
¾" × 1⅜"
11/16" × 1⅜"
¾" × 1"

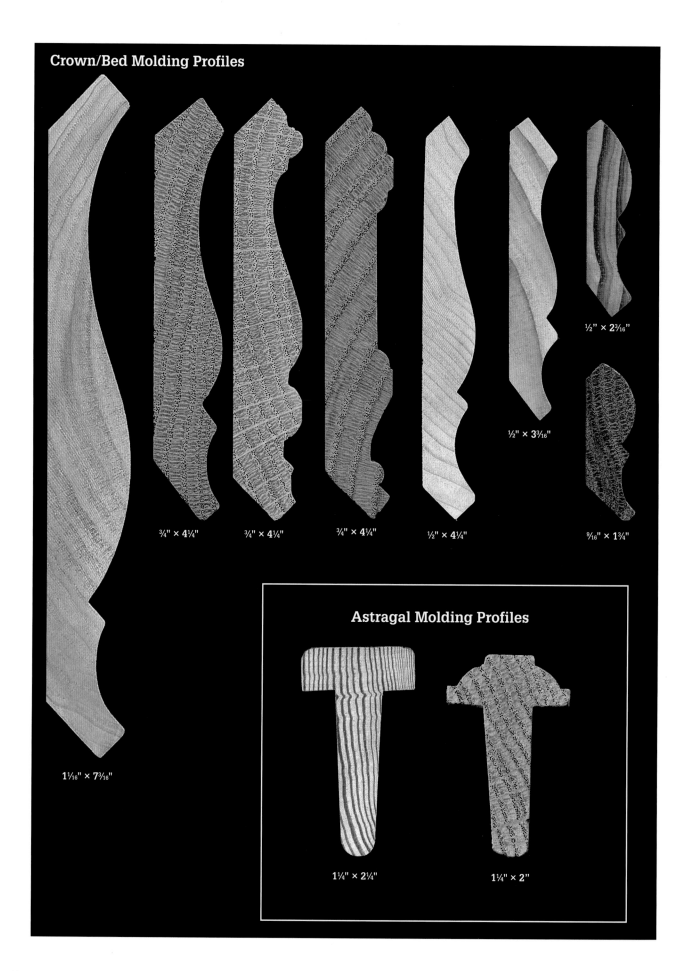

Crown/Bed Molding Profiles

½" × 2³⁄₁₆"

½" × 3³⁄₁₆"

¾" × 4¼"

¾" × 4¼"

¾" × 4¼"

½" × 4¼"

⁹⁄₁₆" × 1¾"

1¹⁄₁₆" × 7³⁄₁₆"

Astragal Molding Profiles

1¼" × 2¼"

1¼" × 2"

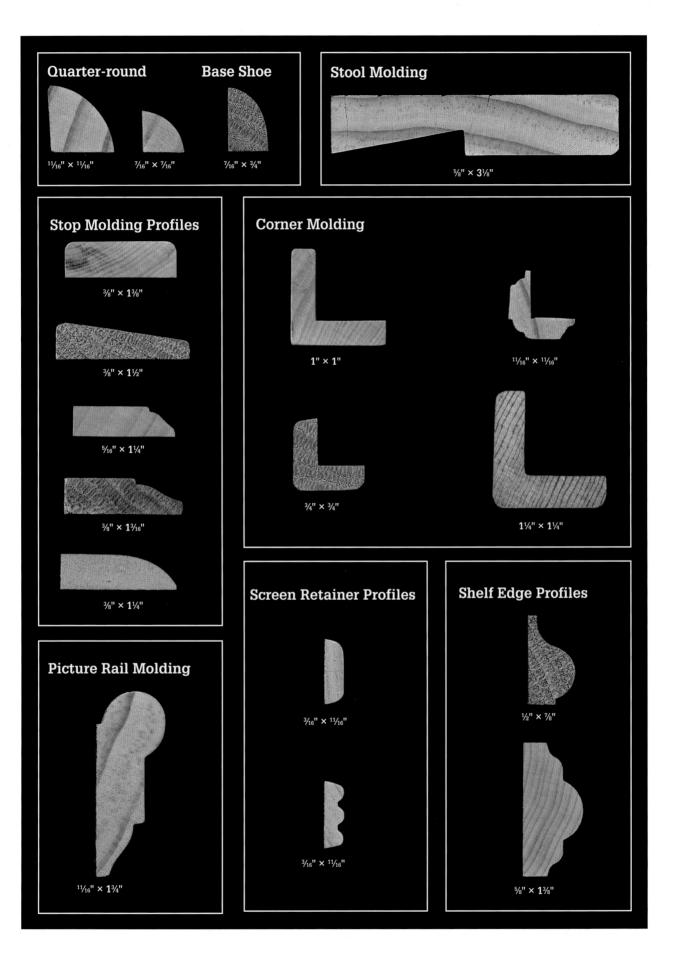

Quarter-round

11/16" × 11/16"

7/16" × 7/16"

Base Shoe

7/16" × 3/4"

Stool Molding

5/8" × 31/8"

Stop Molding Profiles

3/8" × 13/8"

3/8" × 11/2"

5/16" × 11/4"

3/8" × 13/16"

3/8" × 11/4"

Corner Molding

1" × 1"

11/16" × 11/16"

3/4" × 3/4"

11/4" × 11/4"

Picture Rail Molding

11/16" × 13/4"

Screen Retainer Profiles

3/16" × 11/16"

3/16" × 11/16"

Shelf Edge Profiles

1/2" × 7/8"

5/8" × 13/8"

Glues & Adhesives

Glues and adhesives are available at any hardware store or home center in many different specialty forms, depending upon the type of application. Use hot glue for lightweight trim projects, carpenter's glue for wood joints, and adhesive for strong bonds between panels or lumber.

Panel adhesive is used to install paneling, wainscot, or other tongue-and-groove materials. Most adhesives are applied with a caulk gun, but some types are available in squeeze tubes for smaller applications. Caulks are designed to permanently close joints, fill gaps in woodwork, and hide subtle imperfections. Different caulks are made of different compounds and vary greatly in durability and workability. Latex caulks clean up with water and are paintable, but don't last as long as silicone-based products. Read the product label for adhesion quality to specific materials and ask a store representative for more information if you are uncertain which will work best for you.

If you are installing a trim project with a darker wood, such as walnut, or your trim has a dark finish applied, consider purchasing dark carpenter's glue for joint application. Dark glue dries at the same rate and with the same strength as regular carpenter's glue, but squeeze out from the joints will be less visible with a dark background. Exterior wood glue has a longer shelf life than regular glue and is a better multipurpose choice.

Polyurethane glue provides a high-strength bond between almost any materials; however, do not overapply. The dried product is difficult to remove from finished surfaces.

Carpentry adhesives include carpenter's wood glue, exterior carpenter's glue, liquid hide glue, polyurethane glue, panel adhesive, construction adhesive, latex caulk, silicone caulk, and a hot glue gun with glue sticks.

Screws & Nails

Screws and nails are the fasteners of choice for trim carpentry projects. Nails are the most common way of fastening trim in place, but screws are used for installing blocking, building up backing material, and installing trim in instances where nails don't have the holding power. Use box nails or long wallboard screws for rough framing of blocking, or backing for panels. For exterior trim projects and fastening door jambs, use casing nails. Finish nails are used for most trim installation because they have a slight head that is easy to countersink and conceal. To install smaller or thinner trim pieces that are prone to splitting, use brad nails. Brad nails are shorter and have a smaller gauge than finish nails for light trim work.

No matter what you are fastening, make sure the fasteners you choose are appropriate for your installation. Approximately half of the fastener should be embedded in the backing material when driven in place. It is a good idea to drill pilot holes in all materials before fastening them. Driving a fastener through wood without a pilot hole can split the wood fibers. These splits may not be visible when you are finished, but the integrity of your trim will be affected. Predrilling eliminates this splitting and creates stronger joints that last longer.

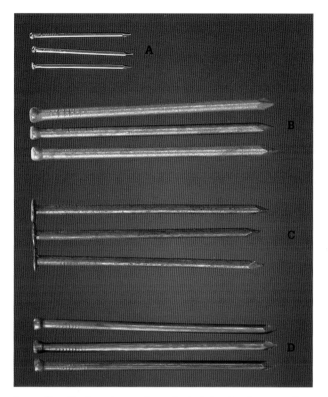

"Hand" nails for trim projects include brad nails (A), casing nails rated for exterior use (B), box nails (C), and finish nails (D).

Use deck and wallboard screws for general-purpose, convenient fastening. Driving options include Phillips drive and square drive. Use trimhead screws to fasten trim to walls.

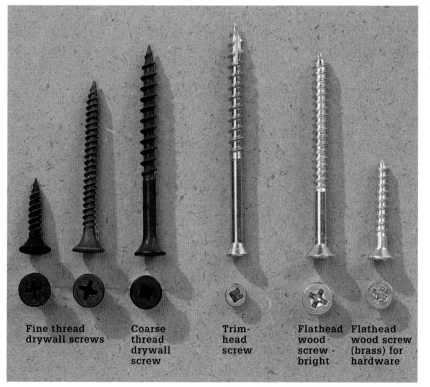

Fine thread drywall screws

Coarse thread drywall screw

Trim-head screw

Flathead wood screw - bright

Flathead wood screw (brass) for hardware

Abrasives

Sandpaper is readily available from any hardware store or home center in a variety of styles, shapes, and sizes for just about any sanding task. Sandpaper is generally available in grits from 60 to 220, but finer and coarser grits are also offered at some locations.

The 60-grit sandpaper is used to grind down badly scratched surfaces and is rarely needed for trim carpentry applications. A 100-grit sandpaper is used for initial smoothing of wood. Stock moldings purchased from a home center or lumberyard may need a light initial sanding with 100-grit paper. Use 150-grit sandpaper to put a smooth finish on wood surfaces before painting or staining material. And 220-grit sandpaper is useful for light sanding between coats of varnish or to remove sanding marks left from power sanders.

No matter what you are sanding, begin with a lower-grit paper and work your way up the grit levels until you reach the desired smoothness for your project. Do not skip grit levels, especially 100-grit paper. Doing so will make it very difficult to remove scratches from previous sanding, and will leave some hardwoods with deep grain marks that will be visible through your finish.

Always wear a dust mask when sanding, particularly when using power sanders. The airborne particles created while sanding can cause serious health problems. The dust from some hardwoods, such as walnut, is known to cause serious allergic reactions in some people.

Random-orbit Sanders ▸

Random-orbit sanders are great for trim carpentry work. Their random, circular motion leaves a very smooth finish that is free from uniform sanding marks. When working with a random-orbital sander, keep light pressure on the sander and move with the grain of the material. Leaving the sander in one place may cause an uneven finish and can possibly wear through a thin veneer. It is important to use sandpaper with the correct hole orientation. The holes (either five or eight) in the sandpaper allow particles to be drawn through the sanding pad and into dust collection ports. When adhering the sheets (some are self-adhesive and some use hook-and-loop fabric), be sure that the holes align with the holes in the sander.

Random-orbit sander being used on a piece of trim.

Sanding block

Precut papers for power sanders

Sheet sandpaper

Foam-backed sandpaper

Sandpaper is available in a variety of styles for various applications: basic sheet sandpaper for general use, sponge sanding blocks for materials with light curves, and foam-backed paper for sanding tight curves and intricate details. Precut papers for power sanders include Velcro or adhesive backing.

Wood Fillers

No matter what type of finish you choose, painted or clear, wood fillers provide a convenient way to fill fastener holes quickly and effectively with minimal sanding or cleanup. Each product differs in some way, including varying drying times, hardness when dry, and adhesion to specific materials. Read the packaging carefully to determine which product will best suit your needs.

Clear finishes require a filler that will either match the final finish color or stain similarly to the trim material. If you will be staining and varnishing your trim after it is installed, consider purchasing filler that will match when stained. Available in solvent and solvent-free form, these fillers apply easily with a putty knife, dry in a very brief amount of time, and sand with ease. Before applying stain-matching filler, use a scrap piece of trim to test the color.

If your trim will be finished prior to installation, use oil-based finishing putty to fill holes. This putty is available in numerous colors that can be mixed to achieve a nearly indistinguishable fill. Finish putty will never harden completely, so it's a good idea to apply one coat of varnish over the top to match the sheen of the finish.

Fastener holes in painted finishes can be filled with two main types of filling material. One is a premixed filler that is normally solvent based, such as plastic wood. The other requires mixing.

Solvent-based premixed fillers generally dry faster and harder than their water-based counterparts. Although premixed fillers are convenient to use, they have a shorter shelf life and are more expensive.

Fillers that require mixing are available in powder form for water-based products and two-part resin and hardener mixes for solvent-based products. Both work equally well in most circumstances; however, two-part resin and hardener mixes may emit dangerous fumes and should be handled with caution.

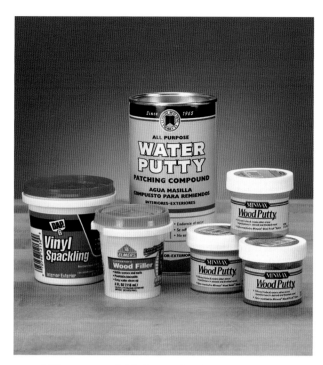

Wood fillers are available for two finish types: painted and clear finish. Based on the type of finish you choose and the fastener hole size to fill, these products provide many options for your filling needs.

Grain filler is available to brush on open-grained woods before finishing. These products fill in wood grain so that it does not mirror through the finish, creating a smoother appearance.

Job Site Preparation

Whether you are installing base trim in an entire house or just improving the appearance of window, with an additional molding, preparing the job site is an important step of your project. Remove as much furniture from the rooms you will be working in as possible so that you won't worry about getting sawdust on a nice upholstered chair or damaging an antique furnishing with a scratch. Cover any items you cannot remove with plastic sheeting. You may also want to cover finished floors with cardboard or plastic as well to protect them from scratches or just to make cleanup easier.

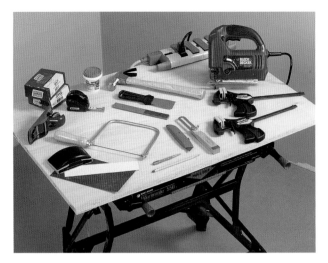

Organize your tools and avoid a bulky work belt by setting up a dedicated tool table where all of your project tools and materials can be staged.

The Work Area

Set up tools such as a power miter saw at a central workstation to avoid walking long distances between where you are installing and where you are cutting material. This central location is key to professional results, because measurements are easier to remember and quick trimming is possible without the added time of exiting and entering the house.

Make sure the work area is well lit. If you don't already own one, purchase a portable light (trouble light) to make viewing the workpieces easier. Keep your tools sharp and clean. Accidents are more likely when blades are dull and tools are covered in dust and dirt.

Keep the work area clean and organized. A dedicated tool table for staging your tools is a great organizational aid. Tool tables also make it possible to conveniently keep tools from disappearing. If you only use the tools that you need and set them on the tool table when you aren't using them, tools stay off the floor and out of other rooms. Add a set of clamps to the table and you have a convenient space for fine-tuning the fit of each trim piece.

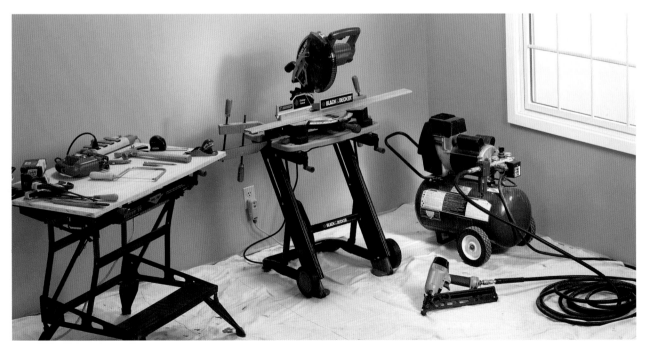

In some trimwork projects, the most efficient way to accomplish the work is to convert the installation room into a temporary workshop.

Project Safety

Personal safety should be a priority when working on any project. Power tools and hand tools can cause serious injuries that require immediate attention. Be prepared for such situations with a properly stocked first aid kit. Equip your kit with a variety of bandage sizes and other necessary items such as antiseptic wipes, cotton swabs, tweezers, sterile gauze, and a first aid handbook.

To help you avoid using the first aid kit, read the owner's manuals of all power tools before operating them, and follow all outlined precautions. Protect yourself with safety glasses, ear protection, and dust masks and respirators when necessary.

Keep your work environment clean and free of clutter. Clean your tools and put them away after each work session, sweep up dust and any leftover fasteners, and collect scraps of cutoff trim in a work bucket. These scraps may come in handy before the end of the project, so keep them around until you are finished.

Maintain safety throughout your project, and remember that being safe is a priority. Everyone needs to use ear protection when operating loud tools. If you don't, you will lose your hearing. People don't just get used to loud noise. They lose their hearing and the noise doesn't seem as loud. The concept that safety applies to everyone but you is foolish. Take the necessary precautions to prevent injury to yourself and those around you.

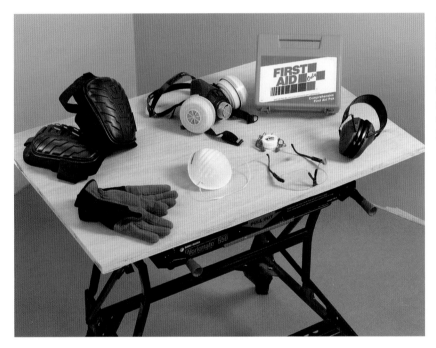

Always wear safety glasses and ear protection when operating power tools. Use dust masks when necessary, and protect yourself from chemicals with a respirator. Work gloves save your hands when moving or handling large amounts of material. Knee pads are useful when working on floor-level projects such as baseboard.

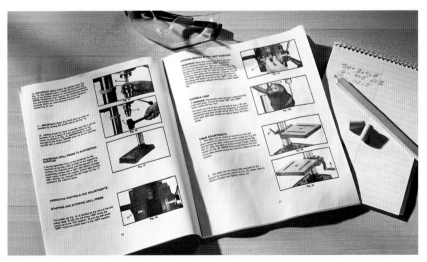

Read the owner's manual before operating any power tool. Your tools may differ in many ways from those described in this book, so it's best to familiarize yourself with the features and capabilities of the tools you own. Always wear eye and ear protection when operating a power tool. Wear a dust mask when the project will produce dust.

Estimating Material

Estimating material is an important part of any trim project. Taking the time to do a quality estimation of your needs will pay off with fewer trips to the lumberyard and little excess material. Estimating materials also helps keep your project in budget as you only buy what you need to get the job done.

Begin by measuring the precise length needed for each piece of molding and marking the dimensions in your scale drawings. When all dimensions are measured, add the total lineal feet together. This number represents the minimum number of feet you need to purchase to complete the job.

To save yourself the difficulty of splicing in materials over every length, you may need to call the lumberyard or home center you are purchasing from to find out what dimensions the moldings are available in. Some moldings are sold in random lengths ranging from 1 ft. to 16 ft. Others are only available in 8- or 10-ft. lengths. When you know the availability of the moldings you want, take the time to write out a detailed list, optimizing the lengths of material with the fewest number of joints.

Similar methods should be used to estimate paint, paneling, and plywood. Make a separate list for every trim element, molding, or sheet good needed. Separate lists help avoid confusion when ordering materials or picking the stock off the shelf. Consider purchasing a project calculator for easier estimating. Project calculators are preprogrammed with formulas for everything including estimating paint coverage, lineal feet for moldings, and calculating to the nearest $\frac{1}{16}$" or better.

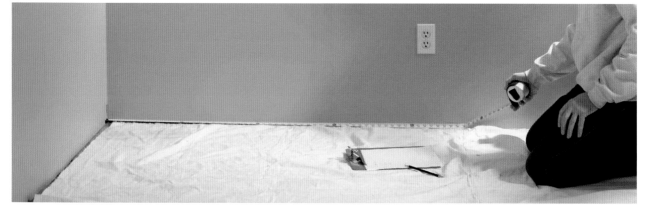

Calculating the lineal, or running, length of molding you need is one of the first steps in estimating your material needs. Take precise measurements, then add 10 percent to account for waste and improperly cut materials.

Project calculators simplify the math of square-foot coverage for paint, panel coverage for wainscoting, and lineal feet for trim components. The model shown calculates in fractions as well making precise measurement addition simple.

Make a detailed list for each trim component, listing which lengths can be cut from a stock dimension. Label the list clearly with the wood molding number and a description of the piece at the top of the page.

Planning a Deadline

Planning a deadline is just as important as buying the material for a trim project. Without a deadline, the other people around you don't know what to expect from the project. Because trim components are cosmetic and not necessary for function of a home, trim projects have a tendency to become drawn out like no other. Planning a deadline gives you a specific point for completion as well as an overall goal to shoot for.

Do not sacrifice the quality of your installation to meet a deadline. Instead, choose a realistic timeline for certain components to be completed, altering the schedule as necessary. Remember that although the project may be exciting and fun now, there may come a time when it begins to feel like too much work. It is at this point that your schedule becomes your friend. No one wants to leave a project incomplete, but you need to make it a priority, or other things will pop up that sound more appealing, and your living room will look like a construction project for too long.

Draw cutting diagrams to help you make efficient use of materials. Make scale drawings of sheet goods on graph paper, and sketch cutting lines for each part of your project. When laying out cutting lines, remember that the cutting path (kerf) of a saw blade consumes up to ⅛" of material.

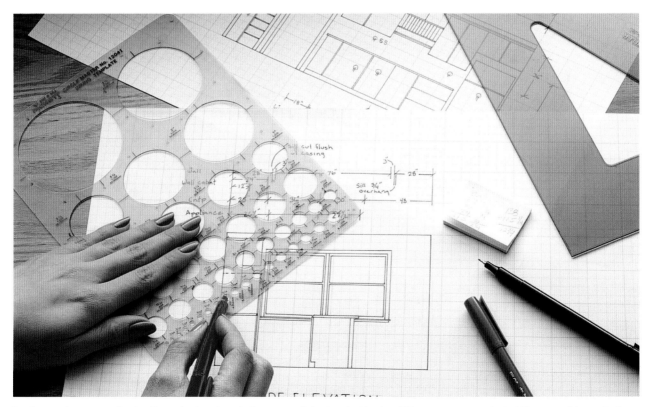

Laying out your project with scale drawings helps you anticipate what tools will be necessary and what the overall impact of your project will be as well as how it will affect your living space.

Establishing Level, Plumb & Square ▸

Good carpenters strive to achieve three basic ideals in their work: plumb, level, and square. Go into any home, however, and you are bound to find walls that bow, floors that slope, and corners that don't form right angles. This doesn't always mean the carpenter did a poor job, but rather reflects the fact that wood and many building materials are natural products that expand, contract, and settle with the seasons. These natural movements do not always occur at the same rate, however, causing fluctuations that sometimes become permanent. That's why it's no surprise that older homes more commonly have larger fluctuations.

These movements can make installing a new trim project challenging. Level and plumb are hard concepts to apply to a wainscot project where the floor slopes heavily and corners float in or out. Compounding the problem further is that power tools are made to cut and shape wood precisely. Preset angles on a compound miter saw don't include angles such as 47 degrees.

In most cases, your installation of chair rail, picture rail, or cornice molding will require compromises. Keep in mind the overall appearance of your project and remember that the concepts of plumb and level are only concepts. Strive to achieve them for quality joints, but don't insist on them when they affect the overall appearance of your project negatively.

A plumb bob is hung to establish a plumb (exactly vertical) line. Plumb can be difficult to visualize. Most chalk boxes can double as plumb bobs for rough use.

Window and door jambs are normally installed level and plumb, but if they aren't, your casing should still follow an even reveal of ³⁄₁₆" to ¼" (about the thickness of a nickel) around the inside edge. Set the blade on a combination square to the depth of the reveal. Then use the square as a guide for your pencil when marking. Install the casings flush with the mark.

Use a spacer block as a guide to install moldings near a ceiling. The spacer will allow you to easily follow any ups and downs of an uneven ceiling, making the trim run parallel to it rather than exactly level.

Install baseboard as close to level as possible, paying attention to areas where a floor dips or slopes over a longer length. In these instances, "cheat" the baseboard as close to level as you can, leaving a gap below it. You can only cheat the molding to less than the height of your base shoe, or quarter round. These trim pieces will cover the gap because they are thinner and easier to flex to the contour of your floor. Cheating the molding will also make cutting miters easier because they will require less of a bevel.

Use a T-bevel to measure for miter-cutting trim on out-of-square corners. Use a piece of scrap 1 × 4 to trace lines parallel to the corner walls. Place the T-bevel so the blade runs from the corner of the wall to the point where the lines intersect. Transfer this angle to your miter saw to cut your moldings.

Planning a Trim Layout

Planning the order, layout, and type of joint at each end of trim you will be installing is an important step before you actually start nailing things down. A good layout plan like the one shown below helps avoid frustration and errors during installation.

Generally, trim installations begin at the opposing wall to the entry to the room. The numbers in the sample layout plan below represent the order in which each piece is installed. Here, the first piece installed is butted at both ends, tight to the finished walls. Trim pieces are added to the installation, working back and forth around the room in both directions back toward the entry. The added trim is coped at all inside corners and mitered at outside corners. All window and door casings should be installed before any horizontal molding that will butt into it. When running cope joints, install all the butt-to-butt walls first and then the cope-to-outside-corners. On occasion, a cope-to-cope may need to be cut and installed. If the molding has any significant thickness at the top, measure from the face of the moldings rather than the face of the wall.

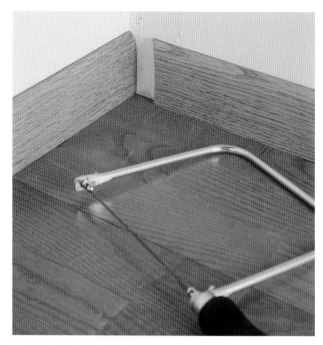

For professional results, contoured molding is coped at inside corners with a coping saw. Fine-tune the cut with a metal file or rasp.

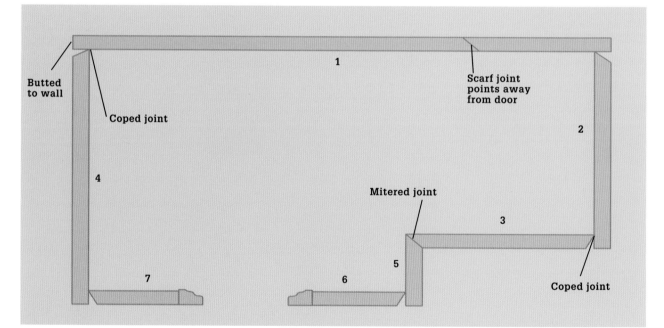

Plan the order of your trim installation to minimize the number of difficult cuts on individual pieces. Use the longest pieces of molding for the most visible walls, saving the shorter ones for less conspicuous areas. When possible, place the joints so they point away from the direct line of sight from the room's entrance. If a piece will be coped on one end and mitered on the other, such as no. 3 above, cut and fit the coped end first. Also keep in mind the nailing points—mark all framing members you'll be nailing into before starting the installation. At a minimum, all trim should be nailed at every wall stud and every ceiling joist, if applicable. Install door and window casing before installing horizontal molding that will butt into it.

Standard Trim Joints

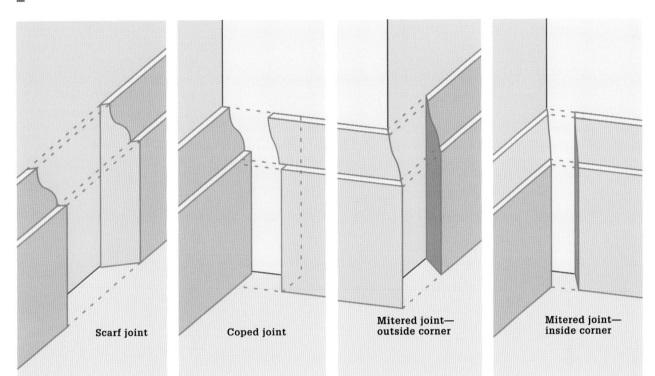

Scarf joint

Coped joint

**Mitered joint—
outside corner**

**Mitered joint—
inside corner**

The basic joints for installing most trim are shown here. A scarf joint joins two pieces along a length of wall. Coped joints join contoured molding at inside corners: the first piece is butted into the corner; the second piece is cut and fitted against the face of the first. Coped joints are less likely than mitered joints to show gaps if the wood shrinks. Mitered joints are used at outside and inside corners. They're typically made with two pieces cut at a 45° angle, but the angle may vary depending on the shape of the corner. Uncontoured moldings can also be butted together at inside corners.

Minimize the number of joints necessary on each wall by using the longest pieces available. Keep in mind that the most visible spaces should have fewer joints whenever possible. Cut all joints so they face away from the direct line of sight from the room's entrance. If a piece will be coped on one end and mitered on the other, cut and fit the coped end first. All nailing points should be clearly labeled before you begin. At a minimum, every piece of trim should be nailed at each wall stud and at every ceiling joist, if installing cornice molding.

If you have never installed trim before or if it is likely that you won't be able to complete the project all at once, consider making a layout plan like the one shown on page 42. There is no absolutely right or wrong order for most tasks, but the chapters ahead dealing with the specific type of installation you'll be doing provide some helpful suggestions about sequencing your project. If you get confused about what to do next, or can't remember where you left off, the layout plan will guide you through the installation.

Miter outside corners, cutting each piece at 45°. Use a pattern with mitered ends to help position your workpieces. Fasten the first piece of each joint to within 2 ft. of the corner, leaving some flexibility for making adjustments when you install the adjoining piece.

Removing Old Trim

Damaged trim moldings are an eyesore and a potentially dangerous splinter waiting to happen. There is no reason not to remove damaged moldings and replace them. Home centers and lumberyards sell many styles of moldings, but they may not stock the one you need, especially if you live in an older home. If you have trouble finding the trim you need, consider looking at home salvage stores in your area. They sometimes carry styles no longer manufactured.

Removing existing trim so that it can be reused is not always easy, especially if you live in a home with intricate moldings. Age of the trim and the nailing sequence used to install it greatly affect your ability to remove it without cracks or splits. Some moldings may be reusable in other areas of the home as well.

Whether you intend to reuse the trim or not, take your time and work patiently. It is always a good idea to remove trim carefully so you don't damage the finished walls, floor, or ceiling surrounding it.

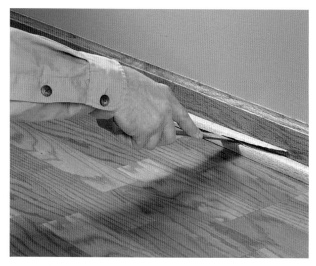

Even trim that's been damaged should be removed carefully to avoid inflicting harm on innocent bystanders, like the baseboard behind the splintered base shoe above.

Tools & Materials ▸

Utility knife
Flat pry bars (2)
Nail set
Hammer
Metal file

Side cutters or end
   nippers
Scrap plywood or
   dimensional lumber
Eye protection
Gloves

How to Remove Painted Moldings

Before removing painted trim, cut along the top seam of the molding and the wall with a new, sharp blade in a utility knife. Cut completely through the paint and caulk between the molding and the wall. If you wish to salvage the material, cut with the knife blade at a slight angle to avoid slipping and cutting across the face.

Work the molding away from the wall from one end to the other, prying at the nail locations. Apply pressure to the molding with your other hand to help draw it away from the wall. A wide joint compound or putty knife makes a good guard to insert between the tool and the wall.

How to Remove Clear-finish Moldings

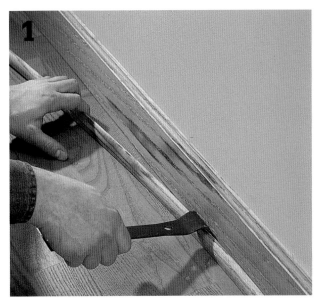

Remove the molding starting with the base shoe or the thinnest piece of trim. Pry off the trim with a flat bar using leverage rather than brute force and working from one end to the other. Tap the end of the bar with a hammer if necessary to free the trim.

Use large flat scraps of wood to protect finished surfaces from damage. Insert one bar beneath the trim and work the other between the base and wall. Force the pry bars in opposing directions to draw the molding away from the wall.

How to Remove Nails

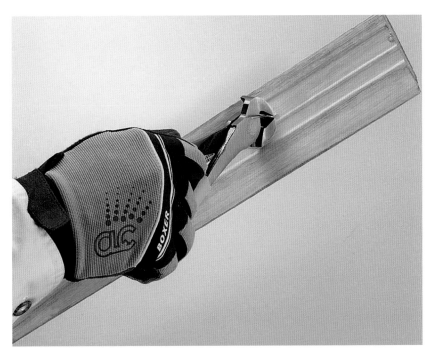

OPTION 1: Extraction. Use an end nippers or a side cutters to pull the nails from the moldings. Take advantage of the rounded head of the end nippers, "rolling" the nail out of the molding rather than pulling it straight out.

OPTION 2: Reversing course. Secure the workpiece with a gap beneath the nail and drive the nail through the molding from the front with a nail set and hammer.

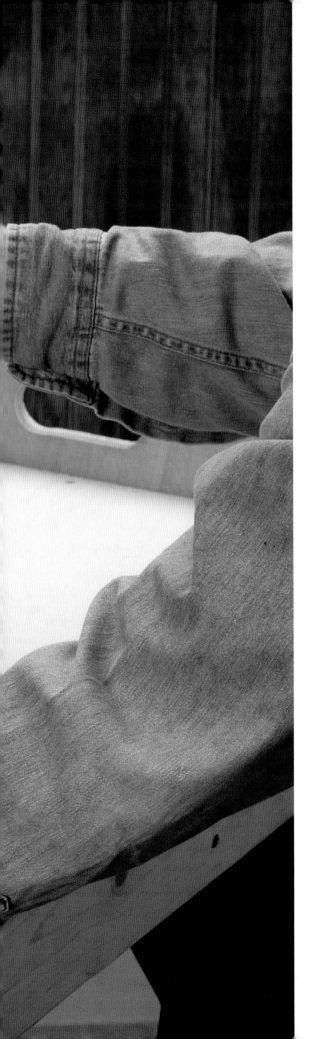

Essential Skills

From nailing base shoe to cutting crown molding, most trim carpentry jobs require the same basic skill set. First (and probably foremost) you'll need to use reliable measuring techniques and apply them carefully to get accurate results. Simply running out the old tape measure and dashing off a couple of rough numbers won't do the trick. You'll need to learn he limitations of the measuring tools you use, as well as some tricks for getting accurate readings in tight or irregular paces.

Taking the measurement is only half the battle: you'll also need to transfer the measurement to your workpiece, either with measuring tools or by using mechanical methods such as tracing. Then you can begin to worry about selecting the best cutting tool and making sure it is set up accurately.

Making the actual cut is not time-consuming, especially if you are using power tools. The best method is to make a creep cut—you secure the workpiece and make a slight cut just outside the cutting line. Then, move the workpiece closer and closer to the blade until it is cutting right on the line. Once you've cut all your workpieces they'll need sanding and perhaps some additional fitting before they are installed. In many cases, it makes sense to paint or finish the pieces prior to installation as well.

This section shows:
- Measuring & Marking
- Cutting & Fitting Joints
- Finishing Trim
- Sanding Trim
- Painting Trim
- Clear-Coating Trim

Measuring & Marking

There are three keys to measuring accurately: taking the measurement, transferring the measurement, and hitting your mark when you make the final cut. The first two keys depend upon proper use of your measuring tools. You can take measurement upon measurement and doublecheck a dozen times, but if you're not using the correct tool techniques, your prospects for success are greatly diminished.

A retractable tape measure is the most important measuring tool for most trim carpenters (although it is definitely not the most accurate). Depending on whether you are taking an inside measurement or an outside measurement, you have to be aware how a tape measure works. The hook at the end of the tape is secured by rivets that allow it to move. The amount that the hook moves is the same distance as the thickness of the hook itself. This allows you to accurately transfer inside measurements to the material you are cutting. When you are measuring an inside measurement, make sure the hook is pushed in. The measurement starts from the outside of the hook. When you hook the tape onto your workpiece, make sure that the hook is pulled out. You are now transferring this measurement from the inside of the hook.

When you are marking your workpiece, use a mechanical pencil or a #2.5 lead pencil. The lead in a #2.5 is harder than a #2 pencil's lead, thus giving you a darker line. Try to make a single line mark. Multiple lines will become fat and you will lose accuracy. For very delicate cuts where great accuracy is required, use a marking knife to score a cutting line.

Tools & Materials ▸

Measuring tape
Clamps
Squared-off fence

How to Measure from a Mitered Edge

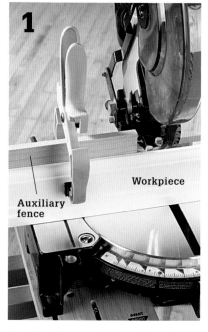

Position the workpiece to be cut against an auxiliary fence on your miter saw so the inside of the miter is flush with the edge of the fence. Clamp the workpiece to the fence.

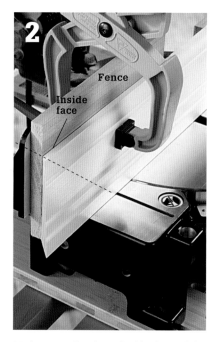

Make sure the short (inside) face of the mitered board is aligned with the edge of the auxiliary fence exactly.

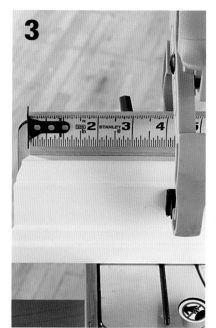

Place the hook of your tape measure against the end of the fence and pull the tape to transfer your measurement to the workpiece.

Using Measuring Tools

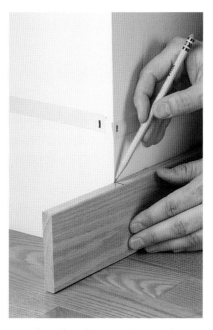

Purchase a well-made 25-ft. tape measure for general trim projects. With the actual fractions printed on the tape, "easy-read" varieties are more user-friendly and help avoid confusion and cutting errors.

Use the trim piece as a measuring device, marking the cut line directly off the wall. Eliminating the tape measure can reduce errors and make it easier to visualize the cut.

To mark a line parallel to the edge of a board, lock the blade at the desired measurement, then hold the tip of the pencil along the edge of the blade as you slide the tool along the workpiece. This is useful when marking reveal lines on window and door jambs.

Use a T-bevel to find the appropriate bevel angle for walls that are out of plumb and for many other angle measuring situations. Tighten the T-bevel and transfer the angle to your miter saw to set up for cutting the molding.

Scribe the back of a molding and check the mark with a square to determine whether or not the corner is plumb. If the scribe mark is not square, transfer the angle to your saw with a T-bevel and make a compound miter cut.

Cutting & Fitting Joints

Cutting and fitting joints is a skill that requires patience, knowledge, and well-maintained equipment to achieve effective results. There are a few basic joints that are generally used for most trim applications: butt, inside and outside miter, scarf, and coped joints.

Although cutting trim joints accurately is the key function of a power miter saw, it is not the only tool necessary for quality joinery. Coped joints require a coping saw as well as a set of metal files. For some trim applications such as frame and panel wainscot, fitting butt joints is simplified with the use of a biscuit jointer or a pocket hole jig. These are specialty tools designed for joining wood.

Cutting and fitting joints during installation can be very frustrating, especially when it involves difficult walls that are not plumb and corners that are out of square. Take the time to read through the proper techniques of using a miter saw, as well as the correct method for cutting each individual joint. These techniques are described in detail to help you work through the imperfections found in every house and to avoid common problems during installation.

The first step to achieving an accurate cut is to set up your saws so they are true. On a power miter saw, check that the blade is perpendicular to the base and to the fence. The second step to making an accurate cut is to ensure that your workpiece is flat on the base and tight against the fence. This will not only ensure accurate cuts but will hold the workpiece firmly in place. Be sure to refer to the manufacturer's instructions when adjusting the saw.

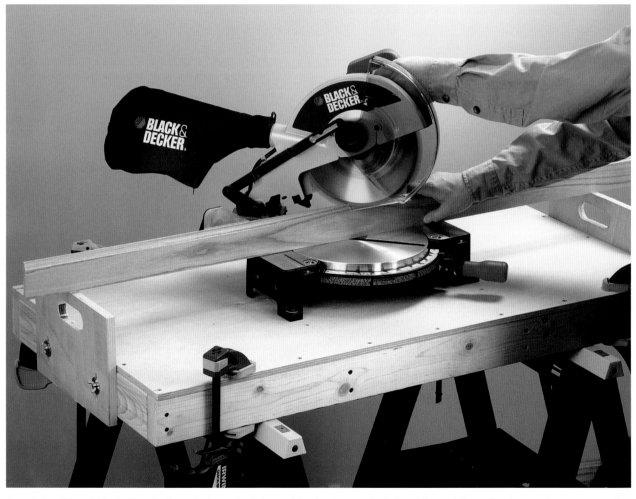

Careful cutting is the hallmark of good joinery, be it for making furniture or installing trim moldings. Used correctly, a power miter saw offers the speed and precision to make your project look like it was done by a pro.

Cutting with a Power Miter Saw

There are two general types of power miter saw. The basic style cuts mitered angles when material is placed against the fence or beveled angles when material is placed flat on the work surface. The second type is called a compound miter saw. Compound saws allow you to cut a miter and a bevel simultaneously. The compound angle is extremely helpful in situations where a corner is out of plumb and a mitered angle requires a bevel to compensate. Some compound saws are available with a sliding feature that allows you to cut through wider stock with a smaller blade size. This option raises the cost of the saw considerably.

Creep cuts. To avoid cutting off too much, start out by making a cut about ¼" to the waste side of the cutting line, then nibble at the workpiece with one or more additional cuts until you have cut up to the cutting line. Wait until the blade stops before raising the arm on every cut.

Use stops on your saw base or saw stand to make uniform cuts of multiple pieces. If your saw or stand doesn't have adjustable stops, or if the workpiece is longer than the saw stop capacity, clamp a wood block to the saw table or worksurface to function as a stop.

How to Cut Wide Stock

With a power miter saw: Make a full downward cut. Release the trigger and let the blade come to a full stop, then raise the saw arm. Flip the workpiece over and finish the cut.

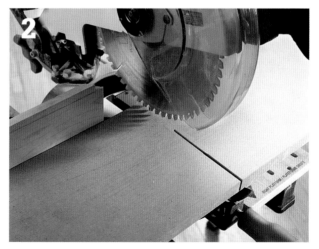

With a sliding compound miter saw: Equipped with a saw carriage that slides away from the fence, these saws have greater cutting capacity than a nonsliding saw so they can cut wider stock. They're also more expensive, but you may find it worth renting one.

Mitering Outside Corners

Cutting outside miters is one of the main functions of a power miter saw. Most saws have positive stops (called detents) at 45° in each direction, so standard outside corners are practically cut for you by the saw. Keep in mind that your saw must be accurately set up to cut joints squarely. Read the owner's manual for setting up your saw as well as for safety precautions. Before you begin, check the walls for square with a combination square or a framing square. If the corner is very close to square, proceed with the square corner installation. If the corner is badly out of square, follow the "Out of Square" procedure on the following page.

Tools & Materials ▸

Combination square or framing square	Air compressor
	Air hose
Miter saw	T-bevel
Pencil	Molding
Tape measure	Masking tape
Pneumatic finish nail gun	1 × 4
	Eye protection

How to Miter Outside Corners

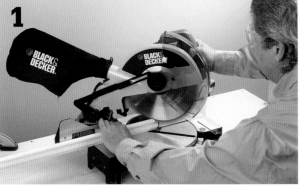

Set the miter saw to 45°. Position the first piece on edge, flat on the miter box table, flush against the fence. Hold the piece firmly in place with your left hand and cut the trim with a slow, steady motion. Release the power button of the saw and remove the molding after the blade stops.

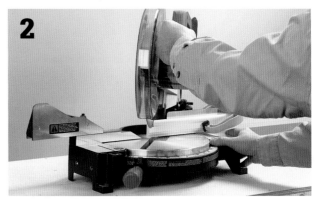

Set the miter saw blade to the opposing 45° positive stop. Place the second piece of molding on edge, flat on the saw table, flush against the fence. Fasten the piece tightly in place with a hold-down or clamp. Cut the molding with a slow, steady motion.

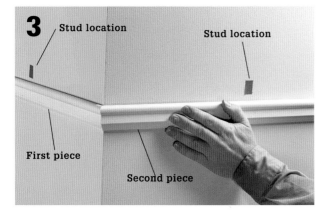

With the first piece of molding tacked in place, hold the second piece in position and check the fit of the joint. If the joint is tight, nail both pieces at stud locations.

If the corner joint does not fit tightly, shim the workpiece away from the fence to make minor adjustments until the joint fits tightly. Shims should be a uniform thickness. Playing cards work well.

How to Miter Out-of-Square Outside Corners: Method 1

Draw a reference line off each wall of the corner using a straight 1 × 4. Put masking tape down on the finished floor to avoid scuffing it and to see your lines clearly. Trace along each wall, connecting the traced lines at a point out from the tip of the corner.

To find the angle you need to miter your moldings, place a T-bevel with the handle flush against one wall, and adjust the blade so that it intersects the point where your reference lines meet. Lock the blade in place at this angle.

How to Miter Out-of-Square Outside Corners: Method 2

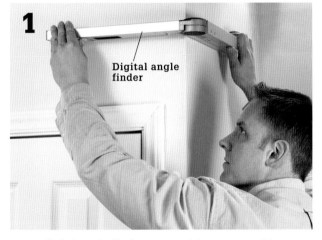

Digital angle finder

Use a digital angle finder to record the exact outside corner angle. These tools are sold in a wide price range, with some costing as little as $30.

Do some math. If the outside corner angle is not a whole number (most angle finders give readings in 0.1° increments), then round up. For example, if the angle finder measures the outside angle at 91.4°, round up to 92° and cut the miter at 44° (180° - 92° = 88° and the miter is half of this, which is 44°). A big mistake is to divide the angle in half without subtracting it from 180. In this case, a 92° angle readout divided in half would yield 46°, which at 2° off the mark would easily cause a visible mistake in the miter.

Mitering Inside Corners

Although most professionals prefer to cope-cut inside corners, it is common to see moldings that are mitered to inside corners. These joints are more likely to separate over time and to allow gaps to show. For that reason it is not advised to use inside corner miters when installing a stain-grade trim product. The gaps will be visible and are very difficult to fill with putty. For paint-grade projects, mitering inside corners makes more sense because joints can be filled and sanded before the top coats of paint are applied.

Tools & Materials ▸

Miter saw	Air compressor
Pencil	Air hose
Tape measure	Molding
Utility knife	T-bevel
Pneumatic finish nail gun	Eye protection

How to Miter Square Inside Corners

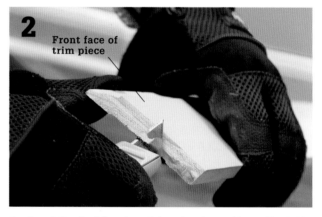

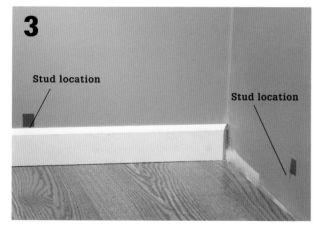

Set the miter saw to 45° and place the first piece of trim on edge, flat on the miter box table and flush against the fence. Hold the piece firmly in place with your left hand and cut the trim with a slow, steady motion. Release the power button and remove the molding after the blade stops.

Back-cut the inside edge of the trim piece with a utility knife so that the top corner will sit flush against the wall corner.

Butt the molding tightly against the wall and tack it into place. Adjust the blade of the miter saw to the opposite 45° angle and cut the mating piece.

Test the fit of the joint, adjusting the miter angle if necessary. Once the fit is tight, nail both pieces at stud locations.

Out-of-Plumb Corner Cuts

Out-of-plumb walls are concave, convex, or simply not perpendicular to the floor and ceiling at one or more points. It is a common condition. In some cases, the condition is caused by the fact that drywall sheets have tapered edges to make taping joints easier and the tapers fall at the edge of a work area where trim is installed. In other cases, the condition may be caused by wall framing issues. In either case, you'll find that it's easier to adapt your trim pieces to the wall than to try and straighten the finished wall surface. To do this, the trim pieces need to be cut to match the out-of-plumb area, to compensate for the taper in the panel. Another option is to install a running spacer along the bottom edge and then to cut your molding square, as shown on the previous page.

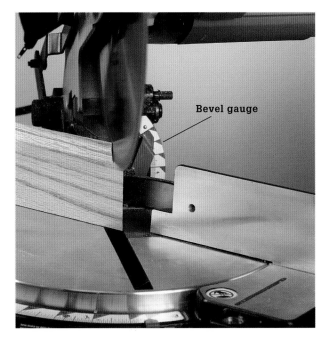

TIP: Occasionally, a compound cut is necessary for cutting miters on out-of-plumb corners. When this situation arises, set the bevel of the miter saw to match the out-of-plumb wall and miter the angle at the appropriate degree. Compound cuts can be difficult to get right the first time, so test the fit with a piece of scrap material first.

How to Make Out-of-Plumb Corner Cuts

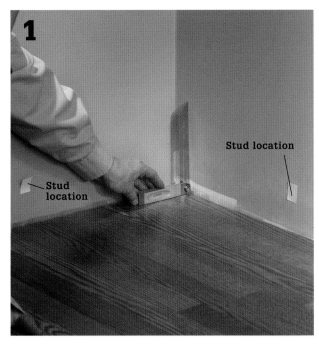

Place a T-bevel into the corner and press the blade flush to the wall surface. Tighten the adjustment knob so the blade conforms to the angle of the profile of the wall.

Transfer the angle of the T-bevel to the miter saw blade by locking the saw in the down position and adjusting the angle to match the angle of the T-bevel. Cut the molding to match the angle.

Making Coped Cuts

At first glance, coping moldings appears to be difficult work that only a professional would attempt. But in actuality, coping only requires patience and the right tools. Whether a molding is installed flat against the wall or is sprung to fill an inside corner junction, as with crown molding, the concept of coping is the same. It is essentially cutting back the body of a trim piece along its profile. This cutting is done at an angle so that only the face of the molding makes direct contact with the adjoining piece.

For beginners, coping a molding requires a coping saw, a utility knife, and a set of metal files with a variety of profiles. The initial cope cut is made with the coping saw and the joint is fitted with a utility knife and files. This fitting can be a long process, especially when working with intricate crown moldings, but the results are superior to any other method.

Tools & Materials ▸

Miter saw	Pneumatic finish
Metal files or rasp set	nail gun
Utility knife	Air compressor
Pencil	Air hose
Tape measure	Molding
Coping saw	Eye protection

Coping is a tricky skill to learn, but a valuable capability to possess once you've got the process down. With very few exceptions, a coped cut can be made only with a handsaw (usually, a coping saw like the one shown above).

How to Make Coped Cuts

Measure, cut, and install the first trim piece. Square-cut the ends, butting them tightly into the corners, and nail the workpiece at the marked stud locations.

Cut the second piece of molding at a 45° angle as if it were an inside miter. The cut edge reveals the profile of the cope cut.

3

Stop cut here

Make the long, straight cut along the edge of the molding. An easy, accurate way to do this is to use a power miter saw set at about a 2° miter. Use a spacer between the workpiece and the saw fence and cut through the workpiece, stopping just short of the profile.

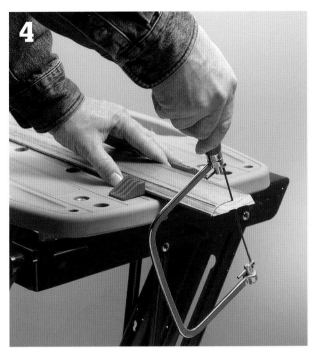

4

The more traditional way to make this cut is to use a coping saw cutting at a 45° bevel. Finish cutting the profile with a coping saw.

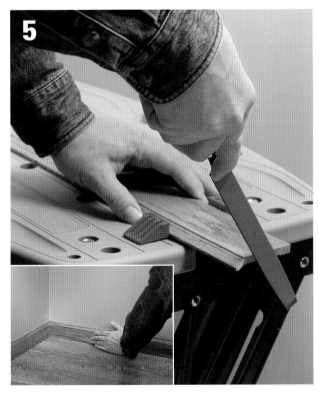

5

Test-fit the piece (inset photo) and use a metal file to fit the joint precisely. When the joint is properly fitted, nail the coped piece in place.

TIP: Trim components such as this chair rail can be complex to cope properly. A variety of rasps or metal files with different profiles is the key to fitting these joints tightly.

Cutting Mitered Returns

Mitered returns are a decorative treatment used to hide the end grain of wood and provide a finished appearance when molding stops prior to the end of a wall. Mitered returns range from tiny pieces of base shoe up to very large crown moldings. They are also commonly used when installing a stool and apron treatment or on decorative friezes above doors.

Bevel returns are another simple return option for chair rails, baseboards, and base shoe. A bevel return is simply a cut at the end of the molding that "returns" the workpiece back to the wall at an angle. The biggest advantage to using mitered returns rather than bevel returns is that mitered returns already have a finish applied. Bevel returns require more touchups.

Cutting mitered returns for small moldings, such as quarter round, or for thin stock, such as baseboard, can be tricky when using a power miter saw. The final cut of the process leaves the return loose where it can sometimes be thrown from the saw by the air current of the blade. Plan on using a piece of trim that is long enough to cut comfortably, or you will find yourself fighting the saw.

Tools & Materials ▸

Combination square	Pneumatic finish
Utility knife	nail gun
Power miter saw	Air compressor
Miter box and	Air hose
back saw	T-bevel
Pencil	Molding
Tape measure	Wood glue
	Eye protection

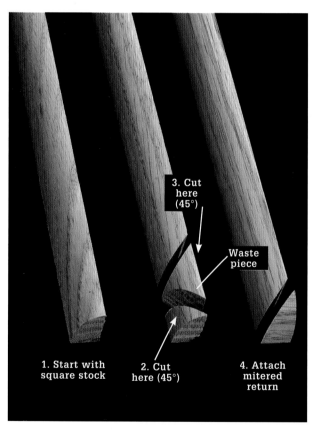

Returns are made from two 45° angle cuts. The scrap piece is removed and the return piece is glued into place.

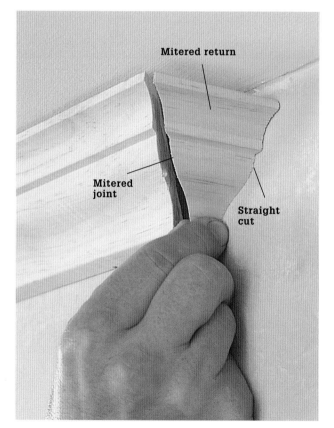

Mitered returns finish molding ends that would otherwise be exposed. Miter the main piece as you would at an outside corner. Cut a miter on the return piece, then cut it to length with a straight cut so it butts to the wall. Attach the return piece with wood glue.

How to Cut Mitered Returns in Shoe

Cut the shoe molding to length, leaving an inside 45° miter at the end that is open or butts against door casing. Install the shoe (always nail shoe to the base trim, not to the floor). The shoe, at its longest point, should be aligned with the edge of the casing.

Mark the return: Cut a piece of shoe with the opposite miter to the installed piece. Draw a straight cutting line across the workpiece so it is the same thickness as the installed piece of shoe. Cut carefully along the cutting line.

Glue the return piece to the end of the installed piece of shoe to create a clean mitered return end that butts neatly against the casing.

OPTION: Instead of making a mitered return, make a partial miter cut to clip the corner of the square-cut base shoe, softening the line where it meets the casing.

Cutting Scarf Joints

Scarf joint is a technical term for the miter joint used to join two pieces of trim over a long length. This joint is not difficult to cut, but should always be laid out over a stud location so it can be properly fastened.

Whenever possible, position scarf joints so they point away from the main entry to the room (or another area from which the joint is most likely to be viewed). Doing so will hide the joint from view at a quick glance.

When forming scarf joints in moldings that will be painted, lightly sand the mating surfaces of the joint to flush out any imperfections, and fill any resulting gaps with filler. Prefinished stain-grade materials need to be tightly fitted and the nail holes filled with putty.

A scarf joint is a glorified butt joint that's used to join two pieces of trim that are the same profile and are in line with one another. Scarf joints are easier to conceal than butt joints and also less prone to opening and showing gaps when humidity or temperature change.

Tools & Materials ▸

Miter saw
Pencil
Tape measure
Pneumatic finish
   nail gun
Air compressor
Air hose
Molding
Eye Protection

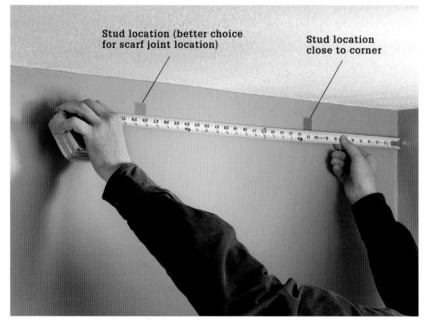

Stud location (better choice for scarf joint location)

Stud location close to corner

TIP: Determine the stud where the scarf joint will be located along the length of the run before cutting any of your stock. Divide the run as evenly as possible while optimizing material yield. In other words, avoid creating a joint too close to the end of the run because it can look unbalanced. Measure the length for the first piece of molding from the corner to the center of the stud location.

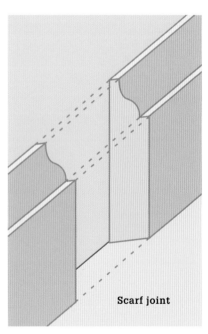

Scarf joint

Any type of molding can be joined into a longer segment with an angled scarf joint.

How to Cut a Scarf Joint

Lay the first mating board flat on a compound miter saw table with the top edge pressed against the fence and the waste portion of the workpiece on the right side of the blade. Make a 30° bevel cut.

Set the second mating board onto the saw table with the waste portion left of the blade. Do not change the saw setup. Cut the workpiece with the same 30° bevel.

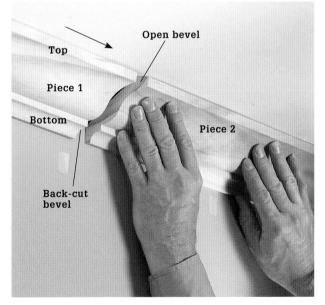

Test-fit the scarf joint on the wall (a helper is a great asset here). Have one person hold the piece with the open bevel (Piece 2 above) in position while the other person places the piece with the back-cut bevel over it. Check for a tight joint and then mark the back-cut piece for trimming to final length. If both ends of the run are inside corners, you'll have to overlap the open-cut piece and mark for cutting to length.

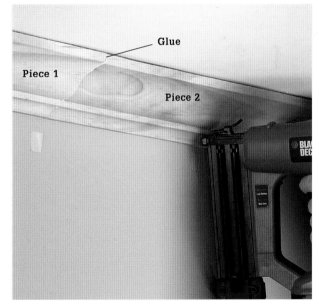

Tack the piece with the open bevel in position and apply wood glue (high-tack trim and molding glue is perfect here) to the open bevel. Re-form the scarf joint and tack the back-cut piece in position. Finish nailing around the joint and then work your way toward each end with the nailer.

Finishing Trim

Even the best trim installation can look bad if the finishing is done poorly. That's why the type of finish and the quality of that finish makes such a big difference in the overall appearance of a room. Often, the finish of a trim project is overlooked entirely or done as an afterthought, and the installer may be so tired of working on the project that he or she does a lackluster job. To avoid this problem, finish as much of your trimwork as possible before you start to install. Paint-grade moldings should be primed on both sides and have one finish coat applied to the face. Stain-grade moldings should be stained and have two coats of polyurethane on the face and one coat on the backside. This way, after the moldings are installed, all you need to do is fill the nail holes and apply a final coat (and sometimes you can get away without the final coat).

Before you buy your material you need to decide what type of finish you will be using. The basic choice is between a painted finish and a clear finish over natural wood.

If you are a novice do-it-yourselfer, consider making your first trim project one with a painted finish. Installing decorative crown molding with a lustrous wood finish might have great appeal for you, but starting out with a painted baseboard installation in a bedroom or utility-type room is more realistic. This project will allow you to practice cutting joints and dealing with trimwork that can be easily filled and puttied, before attempting the more difficult stain-grade project.

Although stain-grade trim projects usually are more expensive and take longer to finish than painted projects, the natural warmth and appearance of wood grain cannot be recreated with paint. Stained projects show off the quality of the trim material rather than covering it up.

To properly prepare your moldings for finish, place them on sawhorses or a workbench where they are easy to reach. When finish sanding, always sand with the grain of the wood, stepping your way up to the coarser grits as you work (each finer grit smooths out the sanding marks from the previous grit). After sanding all the pieces smooth, wipe them down with a dry cloth (or better yet, a tack cloth) to remove dust.

After applying each coat of polyurethane, primer, or paint, examine each piece of trim for surface problems like dribbles, pooling, or skip marks. These areas need to be dealt with in a timely fashion so they do not telegraph through the final coat.

Regardless of the type of finish you choose, take the time to prepare and properly finish your moldings. In the end, you'll be glad you did—your trim will look better and the overall quality of your installation will improve.

Prefinish your moldings. Always apply one coat to the backs of the moldings to seal the entire piece and help balance wood movement.

Finishing Trimwork

Painted trim projects are easier for the novice do-it-yourselfer because nail holes and gaps in joinery (and other mistakes) are easier to conceal.

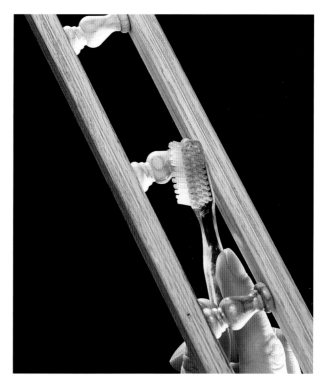

Use a soft toothbrush to apply brush-on finishes to hard-to-reach areas, like spindle-and-rail moldings and other ornamental trim pieces.

Gently but thoroughly stir clear topcoating products like polyurethane before and during application. Do not shake the product or air bubbles will develop in the liquid, leaving burst marks behind on the finished surface.

1. Attach waxed paper to wall before trim is nailed.

2. Pull waxed paper out after trim finish is applied and dry.

If you don't have time to prefinish your casings before installing, tape waxed paper to the walls before attaching the trim. Then when you apply your finish, the walls will already be masked off. Lap the seams so that any drips on the paper stay off the wall.

Sanding Trim

No matter what type of finish you apply, every piece of wood furniture requires sanding to ensure a smooth surface. Preparing trim pieces to accept stain, primer, or polyurethane is essentially the same process. The only difference is at which grit level you call the sanding complete.

Before you start sanding, do a visual check of each trim piece. Inspect the edges for splintering. Most splintering is easily sanded smooth, but larger splinters may need to be glued down. If you're installing clear-finished trim, look for large imperfections in the wood. The sections of trim containing these blemishes should not be used whenever possible. Mark the area of the molding around the blemish with pencil lines, and don't bother to sand it.

Most factory-made moldings are smooth enough off the shelf to start sanding at 100- or 120-grit. Grits below 100 are generally made for rough material removal, not sanding smooth. Trim used in painted projects generally is ready for primer after sanding at 120-grit. Stain-grade projects look better when the wood is sanded up to 150- or 180-grit.

Remember that the purpose behind sanding is to remove marks left from the machining process and leave a smooth surface to finish. Be careful to avoid rounding over the edges and any joint surfaces.

Choose tools and methods for sanding your trim pieces and use them consistently for all grit levels. Sand the trim with long, even strokes running in the grain direction, and reposition the paper frequently to expose new grit to the material. When you are finished sanding, wipe the pieces down with a dry cloth or tack cloth before applying the finish.

Use foam-backed sandpaper for curved or intricate trim pieces to avoid sanding down the high points of the molding.

Mark large blemishes with a pencil, designating them as scrap material. Don't bother to sand these areas smooth.

Sanding Trim

Repair large splinters with wood glue. Use masking tape to "clamp" the piece until the glue sets. Then remove the tape and sand the area smooth to remove excess glue.

Use a sanding block to smooth out flat surfaces evenly. Sanding blocks can also be made from scrap wood, such as a 2 × 4.

Wipe away the dust after the final sanding with a clean, dry cloth. Inspect the face of each piece one final time before applying the finish.

Sand very lightly between finish coats with 220-grit paper. This scratches the surface just enough for the next coat to adhere properly and also removes minor imperfections in the first finish coat.

Painting Trim

Paint-grade trim projects are easier to complete when the moldings have been prefinished. Although you will still need to apply the final topcoat after installation, this simplified method ensures that paint goes on evenly and helps avoid paint marks on finished walls and ceilings.

In their rush to get going on a trim project, many do-it-yourselfers completely skip coating the trim with primer and move right to finish paint. Primer is important. It creates a stronger bond with the raw material than paint alone, greatly reducing cracking and bubbling of the top coats. Primer also costs less than good-quality finish paint and can be tinted to match the finish color, reducing the number of necessary finish coats.

Trimwork is generally primed on both the front and back to seal the entire piece, balancing the wood movement from humidity and temperature changes. After the primer is dry, two finish coats are applied to the face. When the finish coats are dry, the molding can be installed. After installation, gaps in joints and fastener holes need to be filled. The final step is to apply a touchup coat to the filler areas.

Use a high-quality bristle brush to paint trimwork. Straightedge brushes around 2" are the tool of choice for many professional painters when painting moldings. Quality brushes have a shaped wooden handle and a sturdy, reinforced ferule made of noncorosive metal. Many also have flagged, or split, bristles with chiseled ends for precise work. If bristle marks are a concern, consider putting an additive in the paint. Paint additives thin the paint without affecting its durability or sheen. The result is a paint that flows on smoother and lays out flatter when dry. Using an additive may require that you apply at least one additonal coat.

After each coat of primer or paint is applied, carefully inspect each piece for drips or clots. These problems need to be dealt with quickly, or they will mirror through the final coat. Remember that multiple thin layers of paint look better and last longer than one heavy coat. Heavy layers will also hide any intricate details or crisp edging, and could possibly make installation more difficult.

Paint trim moldings with a higher-sheen paint than the surrounding walls. Paint with higher gloss is more durable and highlights the trim, drawing attention to interesting details.

Pour a paint additive into the mix to reduce brush marks on the finished product. A "cut bucket" like the one above is easier to handle than a gallon pail and creates a convenient way to mix the products.

Painting Trim

Dip the brush into the paint, loading one-third to one-half of its bristle length. Tap the bristles against the inside of the can to remove excess paint. Do not drag the bristles against the top edge, or rub them against the lip of a one-gallon can.

Paint moldings with thin, even coats starting along the deeper grooves of the trim, and moving on to the smooth areas. This sequence will minimize drips into the detail of the molding.

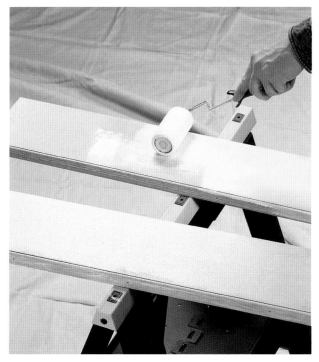

Use a small paint roller to coat long, straight strips of trim material. Rollers make for fast work and don't leave brush marks. If the paint is too thick or you roll too quickly, however, the roller can crate an orange peel effect that you may not like.

Clean the brush with mineral spirits when using oil-based paint, or with warm water when using water-based. Shake out the brush and let it dry. Always start subsequent coats with a clean, dry brush.

Clear-Coating Trim

Water-based and oil-based finishes have a few basic differences in application and results that you should be aware of so that you can make the best decision about which product is right for you.

Not long ago, oil-based polyurethanes were regarded as much more durable and capable of providing more even coverage than water-based products. Today, this is not always the case. The major differences between modern oil and water urethanes are not related to finish quality as much as secondary (but important) characteristics such as odor, finish appearance, and drying times. The durability of water-based products is no longer an issue. In fact, the most durable urethanes available are water-based.

Oil products emit fumes during drying that can linger for weeks. Pregnant women and young children should avoid these fumes altogether. Water-based products create minimal fumes and are not dangerous under normal conditions with adequate ventilation.

According to most manufacturers, water-based products offer faster drying times than oil varieties. This literally means less time spent between coats. Water-based urethanes also clean up with soap and warm water, rather than mineral spirits. Easy cleanup can come in handy for large spills.

The biggest factor to consider when choosing a type of polyurethane is finish appearance. Although water-based products offer many more conveniences than oil, the results can be quite different. When oil-based urethanes are applied, they add a warm amber color to trimwork that creates more visual depth and variety.

Water-based products dry crystal clear. The color of the trim before the product is applied is similar to the finished product. Only a light color change appears. Keep in mind that most of the clear-finished trim in an older house is oil-based and water-based finishes will not match.

The following examples run through the steps of successful clear-coat finishing. These steps are a guideline to finishing only. Always follow the manufacturer's specific application directions. Drying times will vary, depending on temperature and humidity.

Tools & Materials ▸

Bristle brush or foam brush
Latex gloves
Stir sticks
Paint can opener
Drop cloth or cardboard
Sawhorses
Plastic bag (optional).
Trim material
Polyurethane
Stain (optional)

Water-based polyurethane over uncolored red oak

Uncolored red oak with no topcoat finish

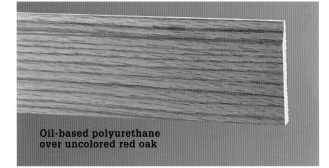

Oil-based polyurethane over uncolored red oak

The finished appearance of oil-based and water-based urethanes often differs. Oil-based products (bottom photo) tend to darken or yellow the trim, which can have the positive effect of highlighting grain characteristics. Water-based products (top photo) offer easier cleanup and faster drying times.

How to Apply a Clear Finish

Set up the work station area with two sawhorses and a drop cloth or sheet of cardboard on the floor. Place the trim pieces to be finished on the horses. Inspect each piece for large blemishes or flaws, repairing any large splinters (see page 65).

Sand each piece as necessary, finishing with a fine-grit paper. Wipe the moldings with a clean, dry cloth to remove any leftover dust.

If desired, apply a coat of stain to the moldings with a foam or bristle brush. For more even coverage of the stain, apply a pre-stain wood conditioner. Follow the manufacturer's instructions for stain drying time, and remove the excess with a clean rag.

Let the stain dry sufficiently and apply the first thin coat of polyurethane with a brush. Stir the polyurethane frequently before you begin, between coats, and during application. Let the finish dry for four to six hours.

After the finish has dried, lightly sand the entire surface with 220-grit sandpaper. This will ensure a smooth finish with a strong bond between layers. If the sandpaper gums up quickly, the moldings need more time to dry.

(continued)

Wipe the moldings with a clean, dry rag to remove any dust. Apply a second layer of polyurethane. Check each piece for skipped areas and heavy drips of urethane. These areas need to be corrected as soon as possible or they may show through the final coat.

Let the moldings dry for four to six hours and lightly sand the entire surface with 220-grit sandpaper.

Apply a third and final coat of polyurethane to the moldings. Keep the third coat very thin, using only the tip of the brush to apply it. Lightly drag the tip across the molding on the flat areas. If the moldings have deep grooves or intricate details, skip these areas; two coats will be sufficient. Try to maintain constant pressure and avoid smashing the brush as this will create air bubbles in your finish. Allow the moldings to dry for a minimum of 12 hours (check the manufacturer's recommended drying times).

Clear-Coat Finishing Tips

Seal brushes in a plastic bag to avoid the necessity of cleaning the brush between coats. Wear latex gloves to protect your hands, especially when working with oil-based products.

Choose a brush that's well-suited for the application. If applying finish to round trim pieces with irregular surfaces, like the Victorian fretwork above, select a brush that's roughly the same width as the diameter of the workpieces.

Always stir urethane products to properly mix them. Never shake them. Shaking creates tiny air bubbles in the product that will follow to your project. Before opening the can, roll it gently upside down a few times to loosen the settled material from the bottom.

Apply urethane in a well-ventilated area. Lack of ventilation or heavily applied product will result in longer drying times. If you use a fan to increase ventilation, aim it away from the project: do not blow air directly on the project or dust and other contaminants will adhere to your finish.

Trim Carpentry Projects

With a full set of trim carpentry skills safely under your tool belt, it's time to get to work. Simpler projects make good jumping off points. For example, install case molding around a window or door. Depending on the method you choose, even this simple project will involve cutting 45° miters—not hard, but if you're off you'll see it right away.

As you gain experience and confidence, tackle some more challenging trim carpentry projects, such as installing frame-and-panel wainscot or adding built-up crown molding to dress up a plain room. Once you've convinced yourself that your tools are not a complete menace to your materials, try upgrading to some hardwood trim stock. It's less forgiving and more expensive than paint-grade trim, but the warmth of real wood is well worth it in many homes.

This section shows:

- One-piece Base Molding
- Built-up Base Molding
- Picture Rail
- Chair Rail
- Built-up Chair Rail
- Crown Molding
- Built-up Crown Molding
- Polymer Crown
- Basic Casing
- Window Stool & Apron
- Arts & Crafts Casing
- Basement Window Trim
- Decorative Door Header
- Wall Opening
- Wall Frame Moldings
- Wainscot Frames
- Raised-panel Wainscot
- Jointless Rail-and-stile Wainscot
- Ceiling Medallions
- Coffered Ceilings
- Custom Moldings

One-piece Base Molding

aseboard trim is installed to conceal the joint between the finished floor and the wallcovering (a necessary feature of a house). Installing plain, one-piece baseboard such as ranch-style base or cove base is a straightforward project. Outside corner joints are mitered, inside corners are coped, and long runs are joined with scarf cuts.

The biggest difficulty to installing base is dealing with out-of-plumb and nonsquare corners. However, a T-bevel makes these obstacles easy to overcome.

Plan the order of your installation prior to cutting any pieces and lay out a specific piece for each length of wall. It may be helpful to mark the type of cut on the back of each piece so you don't have any confusion during the install.

Locate all studs and mark them with painter's tape 6" higher than your molding height. If you need to make any scarf joints along a wall, make sure they fall on the center of a stud. Before you begin nailing trim in place, take the time to pre-finish the moldings. Doing so will minimize the cleanup afterward.

Tools & Materials ▶

Pencil
Tape measure
Power miter saw
T-bevel
Coping saw
Metal file set

Pneumatic finish nail gun & compressor.
Moldings
Pneumatic fasteners
Carpenter's glue
Finishing putty
Eye protection

Baseboard doesn't need to be fancy to be effective. Without a shoe or a cap, a plain, one-piece base molding makes a neat transition from floor to wall.

How to Install One-piece Base Molding

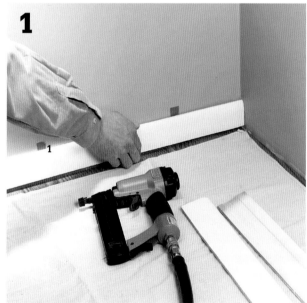

1

Measure, cut, and install the first piece of baseboard. Butt both ends into the corners tightly. For longer lengths, it is a good idea to cut the piece slightly oversized (up to 1/16" on strips over 10 ft. long) and "spring" it into place. Nail the molding in place with two nails at every stud location.

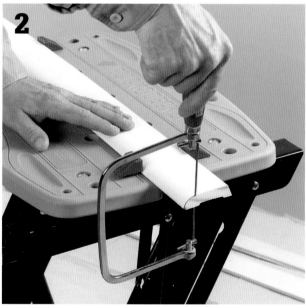

2

Cut the second piece of molding oversized by 6" to 10" and cope-cut the adjoining end to the first piece. Fine-tune the cope with a metal file and sandpaper. Dry fit the joint adjusting it as necessary to produce a tight-fitting joint.

3

Check the corner for square with a framing square. If necessary, adjust the miter cut of your saw. Use a T-bevel to transfer the proper angle. Cut the second piece (coped) to length and install it with two nails at each stud location.

4

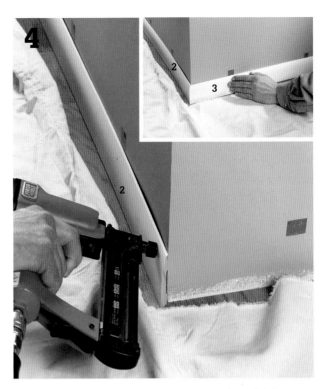

Adjust the miter angle of your saw to cut the adjoining outside corner piece. Test fit the cut to ensure a tight joint (inset photo). Remove the mating piece of trim and fasten the first piece for the outside corner joint.

5

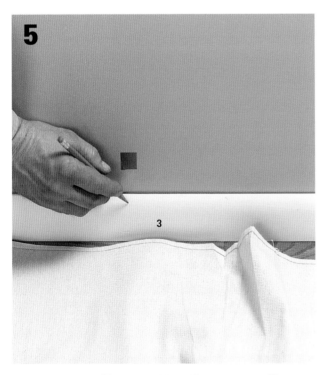

Lay out any scarf joints by placing the piece in position so that the previous joint is tight, and then marking the center of a stud location nearest the opposite end. Set the angle of your saw to a 30° angle and cut the molding at the marked location (see pages 80 to 81).

6

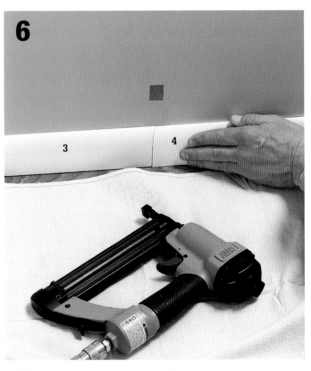

Nail the third piece in place, making sure the outside corner joint is tight. Cut the end of the fourth piece to match the scarf joint angle and nail it in place with two nails at each stud location. Add the remaining pieces of molding, fill the nail holes with putty, and apply a final coat of finish.

Built-up Base Molding

Built-up base molding is made up of several strips of wood (usually three) that are combined for a particular effect. It is installed in two common scenarios: (1) to match existing trim in other rooms of a house or (2) to match a stock one-piece molding that is not available.

Installing a built-up base molding is no more difficult than a standard one-piece molding, because the same installation techniques are used. However, built-up base molding offers a few advantages over standard stock moldings. Wavy floors and walls are easier to conceal, and the height of the molding is completely up to you, making heat registers and other obstructions easier to deal with.

In this project, the base molding is made of high-grade plywood rather than solid stock lumber. Plywood is more economical and dimensionally stable than solid lumber and can be built up to any depth, as well as cut down to any height. Keep in mind that plywood molding is less durable than solid wood and is only available in 8-and 10-ft. lengths, making joints more frequent.

Tools & Materials ▸

Pneumatic finish nail gun	Pencil
Air compressor	Tape measure
Air hose	Sandpaper
Miter saw	Power sander
Hammer	¾" finish-grade oak plywood
Nail set	Base shoe molding
Tablesaw or straight edge guide and circular saw	Cap molding
	2" finish nails, wood putty
	Eye protection

Built-up base trim is made by combining baseboard, base shoe, and another molding type, typically cap molding.

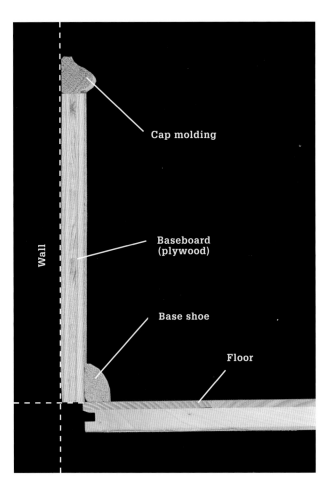

Cap molding

Wall

Baseboard
(plywood)

Base shoe

Floor

Cut the plywood panel into 6" strips with a tablesaw or a straightedge guide and a circular saw. Lightly sand the strips, removing any splinters left from the saw. Then apply the finish of your choice to the moldings and the plywood strips.

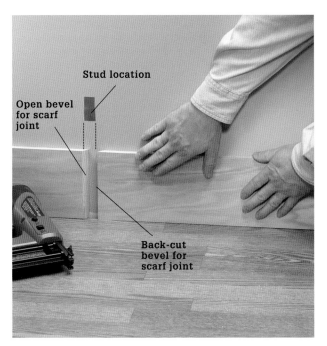

Stud location

Open bevel
for scarf
joint

Back-cut
bevel for
scarf joint

Install the plywood strips with 2" finish nails driven at stud locations. Use scarf joints on continuous runs, driving pairs of fasteners into the joints. Cut and install moldings so that all scarf joints fall at stud locations.

Base Trim Spacers ▶

Baseboard can be built up on the back with spacer strips so it will project farther out from the wall. This can allow you to match existing casings or to create the impression of a thicker molding. However, the cap rail needs to be thick enough to cover the plywood edge completely or the core of the panel may be visible.

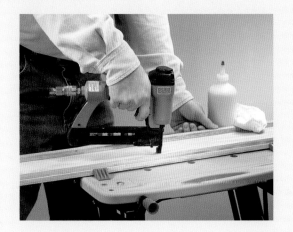

Installing Built-up Base Molding

Test-fit inside corner butt joints before cutting a workpiece. If the walls are not square or straight, angle or bevel the end cut a few degrees to fit the profile of the adjoining piece. The cap molding will cover any gaps at the top of the joint. See illustration, page 76.

Nail and glue 45° outside miter joint before attaching baseboard

Miter outside corners squarely at 45°. Use wood glue and 1¼" brad nails to pull the mitered pieces tight, and then nail the base to the wall at stud locations with 2" finish nails. Small gaps at the bottom or top of the base molding will be covered with cap or base shoe.

Use a brad nailer with 18-gauge, ⅝" brads to install the cap and base shoe moldings along the edges of the plywood base. Fit scarf joints on longer lengths, coped joints on inside corners, and miter joints on outside corners. Stagger the seams so that they do not line up with the base molding seams. Set any protruding nails with a nail set and fill all nail holes with putty.

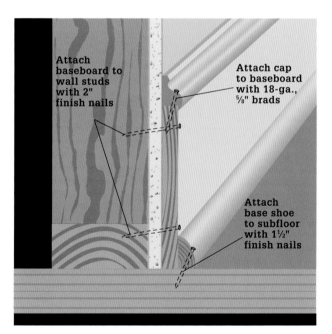

Attach baseboard to wall studs with 2" finish nails

Attach cap to baseboard with 18-ga., ⅝" brads

Attach base shoe to subfloor with 1½" finish nails

Built-up baseboard requires more attention to the nailing schedule than simple one-piece baseboards. The most important consideration (other than making sure your nails are all driven into studs or other solid wood), is that the base shoe must be attached to the floor, while the baseboard is attached to the wall. This way, as the gap between the wall and floor changes, the parts of the built-up molding can change with them.

Options with Heat Registers

Installing base molding around heat registers and cold-air returns can sometimes be challenging. Register thickness and height vary, complicating installation.

Here are a few methods that can be employed for trimming around these obstructions.

Adjust the height of your baseboard to completely surround the heat register opening. Then cut a pocket out of the base for the heat register to slide into. Install the base shoe and cap trim molding continuously across the edges of the base board.

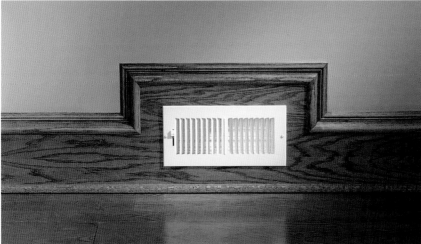

Install a taller backer block to encompass larger register openings. Cut a hole the same size as the duct opening in the backer block and cover the edges of the plywood with cap rail, mitering the rail at the corners. Butt the base molding into the sides of the register. Cut and install returns for the base shoe flush with the ends of the register.

Install a wooden heat register for a less noticeable appearance. Wooden registers can be finished to match your trim and are available through most hardwood floor retailers. Butt the base molding into the ends of the register cover and bevel the front edges of the base shoe to match the depth of the register.

Picture Rail

Picture rail molding is a specialty molding that was installed in many older homes so the homeowners could avoid making nail holes in the finished walls. Picture rail molding is a simple but elegant way to add style to any room. Special picture hanging hooks slide over the molding and artwork may be hung with a cord over the hook. Picture rail molding also provides its own decorative touch, breaking up the vertical lines from floor to ceiling. For this reason, it is also installed as a decorative touch by itself.

Picture rail molding is easy to install but should be reinforced with screws, not brads or nails, especially if you are hanging large, heavy items. Depending on the style of your home, picture rail can be hung anywhere from 1 ft. to a few inches down from the ceiling. In some homes, picture rail is added just below the cornice or crown molding for an additional layer of depth. When applied this way, it is commonly referred to as a "sub-rail."

In the example shown, the picture rail is installed using a level line to maintain height. If your ceiling is uneven, you may choose to install picture rail a set distance from the ceiling to avoid an uneven appearance.

Tools & Materials ▸

Ladder	4-ft. level or laser level
Pencil	Drill with bits
Stud finder	Painter's tape
Tape measure	Moldings
Power miter saw	Pneumatic fasteners
T-bevel	1⅝" drywall screws
Pneumatic finish nail gun & compressor	Hole filler
	Eye protection

Picture rail may still be used as a support strip for hanging artwork, although more often it is installed solely for its decorative appeal.

How to Install Picture Rail Molding

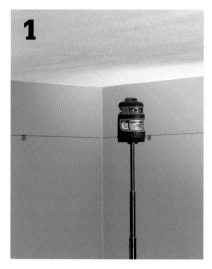

Measure down the desired distance from the ceiling and draw a level reference line around the room using a pencil and a 4-ft. level or use a laser level. Use a stud finder to locate the framing members, and mark the locations on the walls with blue painter's tape.

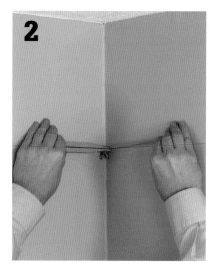

Use a T-bevel to measure the angle of the corner, tightening the lock nut with the blade and the handle on the reference line. Place the T-bevel on the table of your power miter saw and adjust the miter blade so that it matches the angle.

Calculate the cutting angle. First, adjust the saw blade so it is parallel to the arm of the T-bevel when the handle is flush against the saw fence. Note the number of degrees, if any, away from zero that the blade location reads. Subtract this number from 180 and divide by 2; this is your cutting angle.

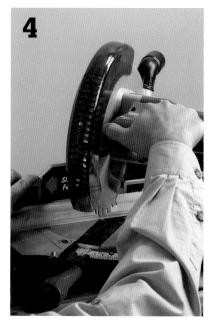

Cut both mating parts at the same bevel angle, arrived at in step 3. When cutting picture rail, the molding should be positioned with the bottom edge resting on the table and the back face flat against the saw fence.

Nail the molding at the stud locations covering the level line around the room (if you're using a laser level, you simply keep it in position and turned on to cast a reference line you can follow). After each molding is completely nailed in place, go back to each stud location and drive 1⅝" drywall screws into the molding through counter-bored pilot holes.

Fill nail holes with wood filler. Let the filler dry and sand it smooth. Then apply a final coat of paint over the molding face.

Chair Rail

Chair rail molding typically runs horizontally along walls at a height of 32 to 36" (the rule of thumb is to install it one-third of the way up the wall). Originally installed to protect walls from chair backs, today chair rail is commonly used to divide a wall visually. Chair rail may cap wainscot, serve as a border for wallpaper, or divide two different colors on a wall. Or more interesting chair rail profiles can be effective alone on a one-color wall.

Stock chair rail moldings are available at most lumberyards and home centers. However, more intricate and elaborate chair rails can be crated by combining multiple pieces of trim.

Tools & Materials ▸

Pencil	Metal file set
Stud finder	Moldings
Tape measure	Pneumatic fasteners
Power miter saw	Painter's tape
4-ft. level	Carpenter's glue
Air compressor	Finishing putty
Finish nail gun	Finishing materials
Coping saw	Eye protection

Chair rail once was installed to protect fragile walls from chair backs, but today it is mainly installed as a decorative accent that visually breaks up dull walls.

How to Install Chair Rail

On the starting wall of your installation, measure up the desired height at which you plan to install the chair rail, minus the width of the molding. Mark a level line at this height around the room. Locate all studs along the walls and mark their locations with painter's tape below the line.

Measure, cut, and install the first piece of chair rail with the ends cut squarely, butting into both walls (in a wall run with two inside corners). Nail the molding in place with two 2" finish nails at each stud location.

3

Miter-cut the second piece of molding with a power miter saw and then cope the end with a coping saw. Clean up the edge of the cope cut with a metal file to ensure a tight fit. Dry-fit the piece to check for any gaps in the joint.

4

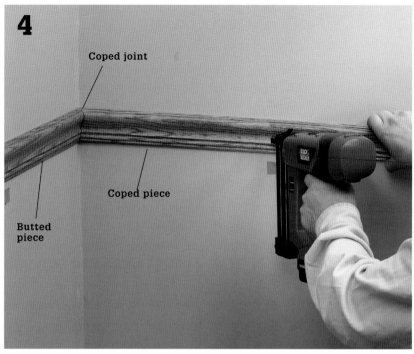

Coped joint

Coped piece

Butted piece

When the coped joint fits tightly, measure, mark, and cut the opposing end of the second piece of trim squarely with a miter saw. Nail the second piece in place with two nails at each stud location. Follow the level line with the bottom edge of the molding.

5

Install the third piece of chair rail with a cope cut at one end. Use a butt joint where the molding runs into door and window casings. Fill all nail holes with putty and apply a final coat of finish to the molding.

OPTION: Apply a painted finish for a more casual appearance. White semi-gloss is a safe choice.

Built-up Chair Rail

Designing and installing a built-up chair rail can be a very creative project that adds a considerable amount of style to any room. For the project shown, five smaller pieces of trim are combined with a 1 x 4 filler strip to create a bold, strong chair rail. If you are considering a larger built-up chair rail, make sure the existing base and crown moldings of the room will not be overshadowed. A good rule of scale to remember is that chair rail should always be smaller than the crown or base.

If you plan to design your own molding, the choices are just about endless. It is a good idea to mimic the style of your existing moldings so that the new chair rail will not look out of place. If the room you are installing in currently has no chair rail, consider new wall finishes as well. Two-tone painted walls will emphasize the transition of a chair rail, as will changing the finish from paint to wallpaper or wainscot.

Tools & Materials ▸

Ladder	4-ft. level or laser level
Pencil	Drill with bits
Stud finder	Painter's tape
Tape measure	Moldings
Power miter saw	Pneumatic fasteners
Coping saw	1⅝" drywall screws
Pneumatic finish	Hole filler
nail gun &	Finish materials
compressor	Eye protection

A built-up chair rail is made of several styles of moldings, so the design options are virtually unlimited. The profile shown here features a strip of screen retainer on top of two pieces of profiled door stop. The stop molding is attached to a 1 × 4 filler that is then softened at the top and bottom edges with cover molding.

Before you begin installing the molding pieces of the built-up chair rail, decide what type of return you will use. Returns are finish details that occur in areas where different moldings meet at perpendicular angles, or quit in the middle of a wall. On some built-up chair rail, you can take advantage of the depth of the molding by butting the back moldings up to the obstructions but running the cap moldings onto the surface.

How to Install a Built-up Chair Rail

On the starting wall of your installation, mark the desired height of the first chair rail component you will install (here, the 1 × 4 filler strip). At this height, mark a level line around the room. Locate all studs along the walls and mark their locations with painter's tape above the line.

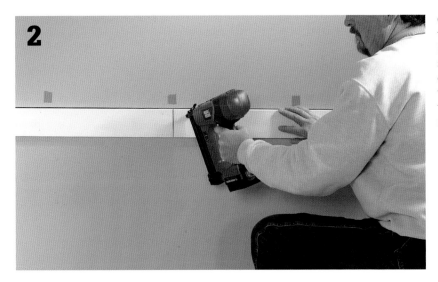

Cut and install the 1 × 4 filler strip so that the top edge of the strip follows the level line around the room. Fasten the strip with two 2½" finish nails driven at every stud location. Butt the ends of the filler strip together, keeping in mind that the joints will be covered by additional moldings.

Cut and install the upper piece of cove molding around the room, nailing it flush to the top edge of the 1 × 4 filler strip. Use scarf joints on long runs, coped joints at inside corners and mitered joints on outside corners. Drive one nail at every stud location into the wall and one nail between each stud down into the filler strip.

(continued)

4

Install the lower piece of cove molding flush with the bottom edge of the filler strip. Use the same nailing sequence as with the upper cove molding. Cut scarf joints on long runs, coped joints at inside corners, and mitered joints on outside corners.

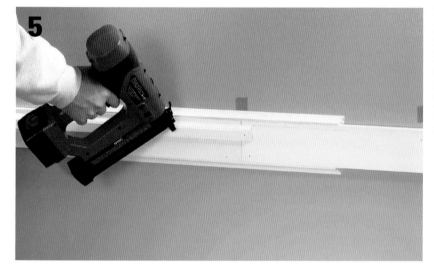

5

Measure, cut, and install the upper piece of stop molding around the room, driving two 1½" finish nails at each stud location. Cut scarf joints, coped joints, and mitered joints as necessary for each piece. Stagger the seams of the scarf joints on the stop molding so that they do not line up with the scarf joints of the cove moldings.

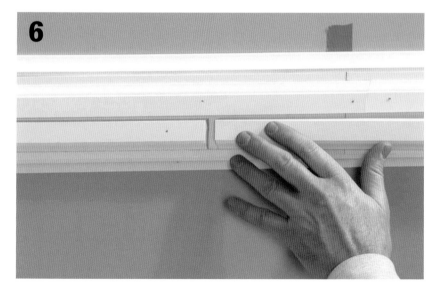

6

Install the lower piece of stop molding around the room, keeping the edge of the molding flush with the bottom edge of the filler strip. Fit each joint using the appropriate joinery method. Drive two nails at each stud location.

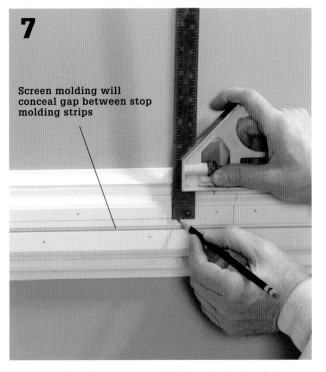

7

Screen molding will conceal gap between stop molding strips

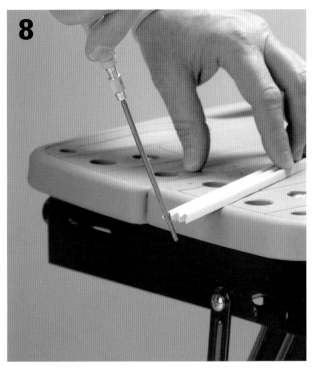

8

Set a combination square to 1⅜". Rest the body of the square on the top edge of the upper stop molding and use the blade of the square as a guide to mark a reference line around the room. This line represents the top edge of the screen molding.

Install the screen retainer molding, as with the other moldings, using the appropriate joints necessary. Fine-tune the cope cuts using a round metal file. Nail the molding in place with a brad nailer and 1⅝" brad nails. Keep the top edge of the molding flush with the reference line from step 7.

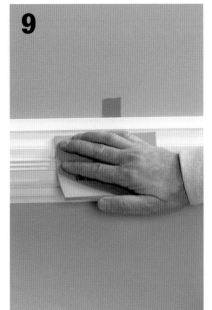

9

10

Set any nail heads with a nail set and fill all the nail holes with paintable wood filler. Check for any gaps in the joinery and fill them as well. Let the filler dry and sand it smooth with 180-grit sandpaper. Wipe the moldings with a dry cloth to remove any dust.

Use a paintbrush to apply a final coat of paint to the moldings. Cover the finished floor with a drop cloth and protect the lower portion of the wall from drips by masking it off with plastic if necessary.

Crown Molding

Simply put, crown molding is angled trim that bridges the joint between the ceiling and the wall. In order to cover this joint effectively, crown moldings are "sprung." This means that the top and bottom edges of the molding have been beveled, so when the molding is tilted away from the wall at an angle, the tops and bottoms are flush on the wall and ceiling surfaces. Some crown moldings have a 45° angle at both the top and the bottom edges; another common style ("38° crown") has a 38° angle on one edge and a 52° angle on the other edge.

Installing crown molding can be a challenging and sometimes confusing process. Joints may be difficult for you to visualize before cutting, and wall and ceiling irregularities can be hard to overcome. If you have not worked on crown molding joints before, it is recommended that your first attempt be made with paint-grade materials. Stain-grade crown is commonly made of solid hardwood stock, which makes for expensive cutting errors and difficulty concealing irregularities in joints.

Inside corner joints of crown molding should be cope-cut, not mitered, except in the case of very intricate profile crown that is virtually impossible to cope (and must therefore be mitered). While mitering inside corners may appear to save time and produce adequate results, after a few changing seasons the joints will open up and be even more difficult to conceal.

Installing crown molding in a brand-new, perfectly square room is one thing, but what happens when the walls and ceilings don't meet at perfect right angles? In most houses that have been around for more than a couple of seasons, walls have bulges caused by warped studs or improper stud placement that's causing the drywall to push out into the room. Ceilings have issues caused by warped joists or drywall that has loosened or pulled away from the ceiling joists. Corners may be best finished with extra-thick layers of joint compound that has been applied a bit heavily, causing an outside corner piece to sit further away from the corner bead. These are just a few of the issues that can work against you and cause even an experienced carpenter to become frustrated.

Tools & Materials ▸

Hammer	Scrap of wood
Utility knife	Eye protection

Basic crown molding softens the transitions between walls and ceilings. If it is made from quality hardwood, crown molding can be quite beautiful when installed and finished with a clear top coat. But historically, it is most often painted—either the same color as the ceiling (your eye tends to see it as a ceiling molding, not a wall molding) or with highly elaborate painted and carved details.

How to Make a Gauge Block ▶

Make and use a gauge block to ensure that crown molding is installed uniformly. A gauge block is used to show where the bottom edge of the crown will sit on the wall. This is especially important for laying out inside and outside corners. To make a gauge block, place the profile of crown upside down against the fence of your saw. The top edge of the crown should lay flat against the base. The fence represents the wall and the base represents the ceiling. The crown will be situated in the same position as it would sit on the wall. Run a pencil line across the bottom edge of the crown. Tape can be placed against the fence to help see the pencil marks. Measure from the base to this line and subtract $\frac{1}{16}$". Cut a block to this measurement and label it to match the profile of crown that you're installing.

Cutting compound miters is tricky. Throughout this book, crown molding is shown being mitered with the workpiece held against a fence or fence extension. This hand-held approach is quick and effective, but takes some getting used to. A practically foolproof option is to use an adjustable jig, such as the compound miter jig shown here.

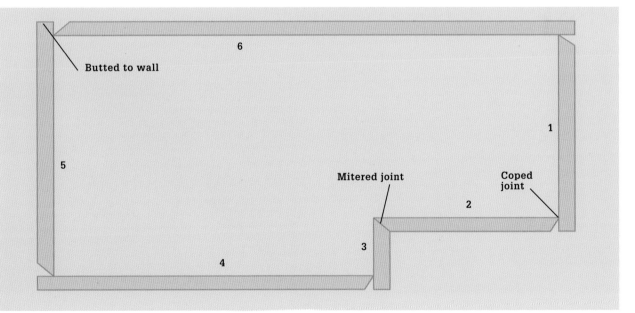

6

Butted to wall

1

5

Mitered joint

Coped joint

2

3

4

Plan the order of the installation to minimize the number of difficult joints on each piece and use the longest pieces for the most visible sections of wall. Notice that the left end of first piece is cope-cut rather than butted into the wall. Cope-cutting the first end eliminates the need to cope-cut both ends of the final piece and places the cuts in the same direction. This simplifies your installation, making the method to cut each piece similar.

How to Use Backers to Install Crown Molding

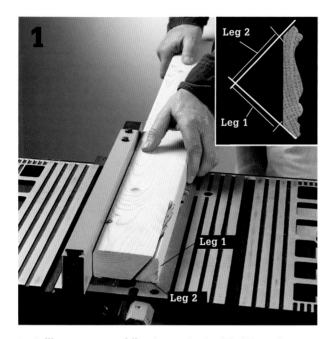

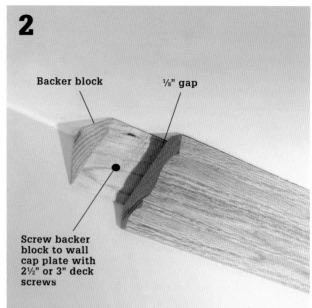

Installing crown molding is greatly simplified if you first attach triangular backers in the crotch area between the walls and ceilings. You can run the backers continuously along all walls or you can space them at regular intervals for use as nailers. To measure the required length for the triangle legs, set a piece of the crown molding in the sprung position in a square in an orientation like the inset photo above. Rip triangular backer strips from 2× stock on your tablesaw, with the blade set at 45°.

Locate the wall studs with a stud finder and mark the locations on the wall with blue painter's tape. Secure the backer block to the wall by driving 2½" or 3" deck screws at an angle through the block and into the top plate of the wall. Now, your crown molding can be attached to the backers wherever you'd like to nail it. Install crown according to the following instructions.

How to Install Basic Crown Molding

Cut a piece of crown molding about 1-ft. long with square ends. Temporarily install the piece in the corner of the last installation wall with two screws driven into the blocking. This piece serves as a template for the first cope cut on the first piece of molding.

Place the first piece of molding upside down and sprung against the fence of the miter saw. Mark a reference line on the fence for placement of future moldings, and cut the first coped end with an inside miter cut to reveal the profile of the piece.

3

Cope-cut the end of the first piece with a coping saw. Carefully cut along the profile, angling the saw as you cut to back-bevel the cope. Test-fit the coped cut against the temporary scrap from step 1. Fine-tune the cut with files and fine-grit sandpaper.

4

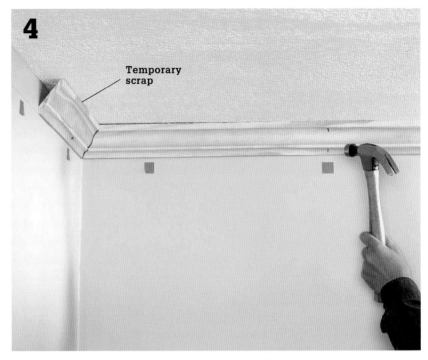

Temporary scrap

Measure, cut to length, and install the first piece of crown molding, leaving the end near the temporary scrap loose for final fitting of the last piece. Nail the molding at the top and bottom of each stud location.

5

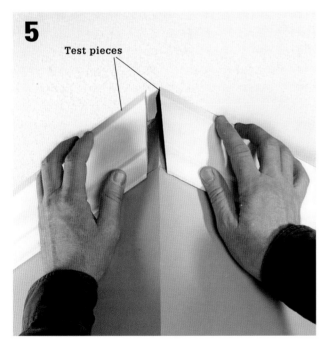

Test pieces

Cut two test pieces to check the fit of outside corners. Start with each molding cut at 45°, adjusting the angles larger or smaller until the joints are tight. Make sure the test moldings are properly aligned and are flush with the ceiling and walls. Make a note of your saw settings once the joint fits tightly.

6

Position the actual stock so a cut end is flush against the wall at one end and, at the other end, mark the outside corner on the back edge of the molding. Miter-cut the piece at the mark, according to the angles you noted on the test pieces.

(continued)

7

Measure and cut the third piece with an outside corner miter to match the angle of your test pieces. Cut the other end squarely, butting it into the corner. Install the piece with nails driven at stud locations. Install the subsequent pieces of crown molding, coping the front end and butting the other as you work around the room.

8

Temporary spacer removed

To fit the final piece, cope the end and cut it to length. Remove the temporary scrap piece from step 3, and slide the last molding into position. Nail the last piece at the stud locations when the joints fit well, and finish nailing the first piece.

9

Fill all nail holes (use spackling compound if painting; wait until the finish is applied and fill with tinted putty for clear finishes). Use a putty knife to force spackling compound or tinted wood putty into loose joints and caulk gaps ⅛" or smaller between the molding and the wall or ceiling with flexible, paintable, latex caulk.

10

Lightly sand the filled nail holes and joint gaps with fine sandpaper. Sand the nail hole flush with the surface of the moldings and apply a final coat of paint to the entire project.

How to Install Crown at a Sagging Ceiling

1

Make light pencil marks on the wall to show where the bottom of the crown will sit. **TIP:** Make and use a gauge block for this (see page 89). This is especially important on outside corners.

2

Score the drywall slightly in the sagging portion of the ceiling. Set the crown along the lines made by the gauge block and the top of the point where the drywall is scored. Mark the edges of the sagging area in a visible spot on the walls.

3

Use a small wood block to drive the sagging drywall up where it meets the wall. Don't get too aggressive here.

4

Instal the crown so the bottom edge is flush with the gauge line. The molding will conceal the damage to the drywall.

Built-up Crown

Built-up crown molding is a multi-piece assembly created by joining several trim boards, usually including at least one crown profile, on the wall and the ceiling. Often referred to as cornice molding, these built-up combinations can be truly striking in appearance, especially at and around outside corners. By using careful layout techniques and building simple mock-ups, this complex-looking process can become relatively simple. In large part this is because the material that is installed both on the ceiling and on the wall can function as a backer, giving the crown molding that's featured in the assembly a secure surface area for nailing. Be creative and experiment with different combinations of trim to come up with a unique design of your own.

Tools & Materials ▶

Power miter saw	Measuring tape
Finish nailer	#2.5 pencil
1½" finish (8d)	Wood glue
or pneumatic	Utility knife
(16-gauge) nails	Eye protection

Buily-up crown molding creates a bit of old-world charm in any setting. The three-piece interpretation seen here is made with two pieces of baseboard and a piece of crown.

Built-up Options ▶

Create a mock-up of the built-up molding assembly you're planning to install. Fasten 12"-long pieces of each type together in the intended orientation. If you are undecided among multiple combinations, make a mock-up of each so you can compare them.

How to Install a Built-up Crown

1

Remove any old crown molding in the cornice area. Use a utility knife to cut through old paint and caulk between the molding and the wall or ceiling. Then, use a pry bar to work the crown molding loose in small sections. Be sure to brace the end of the pry bar on the inside of the crown and pull downward. Do not pry upwards – this can damage the ceiling.

2

Use a mock-up of the built-up molding as a marking gauge to establish a baseline for the bottom of the assembly on the wall. Start in the corners and work your way around the room. This will allow you to see how the ceiling rises and falls so you know where to install the first piece.

3

Make a reference line for the top of the built-up assembly, using the mock-up as a gauge.

TIP: To measure a wall when working alone, first make a mark on the wall or ceiling exactly 10" out from one corner. Then, press the tab against the wall at the other end, measure to the marked line, and add 10" to the measurement.

(continued)

4

Install the base (lowest) molding around the entire room first. The bottoms of the base pieces should be flush against the bottom line that was scribed using the mock-up as a gauge. Do not try and push the trim up against the ceiling—it must be flush with the base line. Any gaps at the top will be hidden by subsequent trim pieces.

5

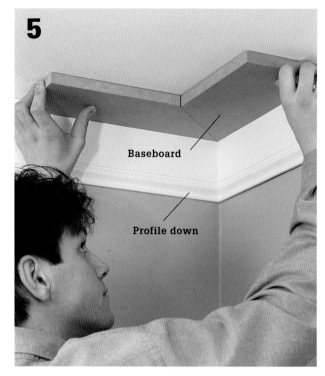

Baseboard

Profile down

Find the correct miter angles for installing the flat ceiling trim. Cut two scraps of stock at 45° and test how well they fit together in the corner. Adjust the cuts as needed to form a corner that has a neat miter with both sides flush against the wall.

6

Install the second trim profile parts all around the perimeter of the room. Typically, this will be flat moldings (with or without an edge profile) installed flat against the ceiling and mitered at the corners.

7

Install the final piece, which is usually crown molding that fits against the flat wall molding and the ceiling molding. It is best to use coped joints at the inside corners (see page 56). Sand, fill the nail holes and finish the built-up cornice as desired (if you have not prefinished all the parts).

Cornice Variations ▸

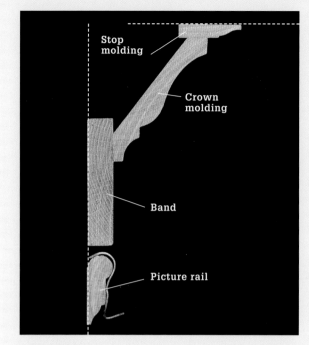

Stop molding

Crown molding

Band

Picture rail

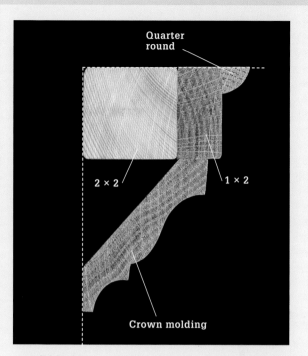

Quarter round

2 × 2

1 × 2

Crown molding

Use picture rail (page 80) to enhance a cornice molding. Standard height for picture rail is about 10" to 12" below the ceiling, but you can place it at any level. For a simple variation of the project shown, use square-edged stock for the band (since the bottom edge will mostly be hidden), and add picture rail just below the band. Be sure to leave enough room for placing picture hooks.

Install blocking to provide a nailing surface and added bulk to a built-up cornice. In this simple arrangement, a 2 × 2 block, or nailing strip, is screwed to the wall studs. A facing made from 1 × 2 finish lumber is nailed to the blocking and is trimmed along the ceiling with quarter-round. The crown molding is nailed to the wall studs along the bottom and to the nailer along the top.

This highly detailed Victorian-style built-up cornice is made of several pieces of stock trim and solid stock ripped down to different widths. The right-angle component of this cornice may be screwed directly to the wall, to serve both a decorative function as well as serve as a nailer for the other trim elements. The screw holes are covered when the crown molding is installed.

Built-up cornice treatments can be as simple or complex as you would like. This Arts & Crafts variation is made of flat solid stock ripped down to specific dimensions. Two pieces of 1 × 2 stock are fastened together to form an L-shaped angle. The angle is then screwed to the wall at the stud locations.

An additional piece of 1" wide stock is nailed in place so the top edge is flush with the installed angle. This configuration creates a stepped cornice with a simpler appearance than the traditional sprung moldings. Notice that the L angle is nailed together with a slight gap at the back edge. This is done to compensate for irregularities in the corner joint.

Polymer Crown

Polymer moldings come in a variety of ornate, single-piece styles that offer easy installation and maintenance. The polystyrene or polyurethane material is as easy to cut as softwood, but unlike wood, the material won't shrink and it can be repaired with vinyl spackling compound.

You can buy polymer molding preprimed for painting, or you can stain it with a nonpenetrating heavy-body stain or gel. Most polymers come in 12-ft. lengths, and some have corner blocks that eliminate corner cuts. There are even flexible moldings for curved walls.

Tools & Materials ▶

Drill with countersink-piloting bit	150-grit sandpaper
Power miter saw or hand miter box and fine-tooth saw	Rag
	Mineral spirits
	Polymer adhesive
	2" drywall screws
Caulk gun	Vinyl spackling
Putty knife	compound
Crown molding	Paintable latex caulk
Finish nails	Eye protection

How to Install Polymer Crown Molding

Plan the layout of the molding pieces by measuring the walls of the room and making light pencil marks at the joint locations. For each piece that starts or ends at a corner, add 12" to 24" to compensate for waste. If possible, avoid pieces shorter than 36", because short pieces are more difficult to fit.

Hold a section of molding against the wall and ceiling in the finished position. Make light pencil marks on the wall every 12" along the bottom edge of the molding. Remove the molding, and tack a finish nail at each mark. The nails will hold the molding in place while the adhesive dries. If the wall surface is plaster, drill pilot holes for the nails.

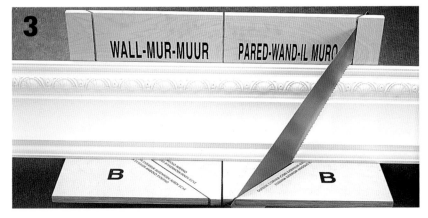

To make the miter cuts for the first corner, position the molding faceup in a miter box. Set the ceiling side of the molding against the horizontal table of the miter box, and set the wall side against the vertical back fence. Make the cut at 45°.

4

Check the uncut ends of each molding piece before installing it. Make sure mating pieces will butt together squarely in a tight joint. Cut all square ends at 90°, using a miter saw or hand miter box.

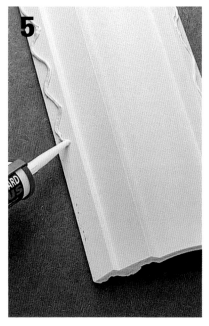

5

Lightly sand the backs of the molding that will contact the wall and ceiling, using 150-grit sandpaper. Slightly dampen a rag with mineral spirits, and wipe away the dust. Run a small bead of polymer adhesive (recommended or supplied by the manufacturer) along both sanded edges.

6

Set the molding in place with the mitered end tight to the corner and the bottom edge resting on the nails. Press along the molding edges to create a good bond. At each end of the piece, drive 2" drywall screws through countersunk pilot holes through the flats and into the ceiling and wall.

7

Cut, sand, and glue the next piece of molding. Apply a bead of adhesive to the end where the installed molding will meet the new piece. Install the new piece, and secure the ends with screws, making sure the ends are joined properly. Install the remaining molding pieces, and let the adhesive dry.

8

Carefully remove the finish nails and fill the nail holes with vinyl spackling compound. Fill the screw holes in the molding and any gaps in the joints with paintable latex caulk or filler, and wipe away excess caulk with a damp cloth or a wet finger. Smooth the caulk over the holes so it's flush with the surface.

Basic Casing

Stock wood casings provide an attractive border around window and door openings while covering the gaps between the wall surface and the window jamb. Install casings with a consistent reveal between the inside edges of the jambs and the edges of the casings.

In order to fit casings properly, the jambs and wall surfaces must be in the same plane. If one of them protrudes, the casing will not lie flush. To solve this problem, you may need to shave the edges of the jambs down with a block plane. Or you may need to attach jamb extensions to the window or door to match the plane of the wall. For small differences where a drywall surface is too high, you can sometimes use a hammer to compress the drywall around the jambs to allow the casings to lie flush.

Drywall screws rely on the strength of untorn face paper to support the panel. If the paper around the screws becomes torn, drive additional screws nearby where the paper is still intact.

Tools & Materials ▸

Tape measure	Straightedge
Drill	Miter saw
Pencil	Casing material
Nail set	Baseboard molding
Hammer or	and corner blocks
pneumatic nailer	(optional)
Level	4d and 6d finish nails
Combination square	Wood putty
	Eye protection

Simple case molding installed with mitered corners is a very common approach to trimming windows and doors. While it lacks visual interest, it is easy to install and relatively inexpensive.

How to Install Mitered Casing on Windows & Doors

On each jamb, mark a reveal line ³/₁₆" to ¼" from the inside edge. The casings will be installed flush with these lines.

Place a length of casing along one side jamb, flush with the reveal line. At the top and bottom of the molding, mark the points where horizontal and vertical reveal lines meet. (When working with doors, mark the molding at the top only.)

Make 45° miter cuts on the ends of the moldings. Measure and cut the other vertical molding piece, using the same method.

Drill pilot holes spaced every 12" to prevent splitting, and attach the vertical casings with 4d finish nails driven through the casings and into the jambs. Drive 6d finish nails into the framing members near the outside edge of the casings.

Measure the distance between the side casings and cut top and bottom casings to fit, with ends mitered at 45°. If the window or door unit is not perfectly square, make test cuts on scrap pieces to find the correct angle of the joints. Drill pilot holes and attach with 4d and 6d finish nails.

Locknail the corner joints by drilling pilot holes and driving 4d finish nails through each corner, as shown. Drive all nail heads below the wood surface, using a nail set, then fill the nail holes with wood putty.

Window Stool & Apron

Stool and apron trim brings a traditional look to a window and is most commonly used with double-hung styles. The stool serves as an interior sill; the apron (or the bottom casing) conceals the gap between the stool and the finished wall.

In many cases, such as with 2 × 6 walls, jamb extensions made from 1× finish-grade lumber need to be installed to bring the window jambs flush with the finished wall. Many window manufacturers also sell jamb extensions for their windows.

The stool is usually made from 1× finish-grade lumber, cut to fit the rough opening, with "horns" at each end extending along the wall for the side casings to butt against. The horns extend beyond the outer edge of the casing by the same amount that the front edge of the stool extends past the face of the casing, usually under 1".

If the edge of the stool is rounded, beveled, or otherwise decoratively routed, you can create a more finished appearance by returning the ends of the stool to hide the end grain. A pair of miter cuts at the rough horn will create the perfect cap piece for wrapping the grain of the front edge of the stool around the horn. The same can be done for an apron cut from a molded casing.

As with any trim project, tight joints are the secret to a successful stool and apron trim job. Take your time to ensure all the pieces fit tightly. Also, use a pneumatic nailer—you don't want to spend all that time shimming the jambs perfectly only to knock them out of position with one bad swing of a hammer.

The window stool and apron give the window a finished appearance while offering the practical advantage of a window sill.

TIP: Back-cut the ends of casing pieces where needed to help create tight joints, using a sharp utility knife.

Tools & Materials ▸

Tape measure	Pneumatic nailer
Straightedge	(optional)
Circular saw or jigsaw	1× finish lumber
Handsaw, plane or	Casing
rasp	Wood shims
Drill	4d, 6d, and 8d finish
Hammer	nails
	Utility knife
	Eye protection

How to Install Stool & Apron Window Trim

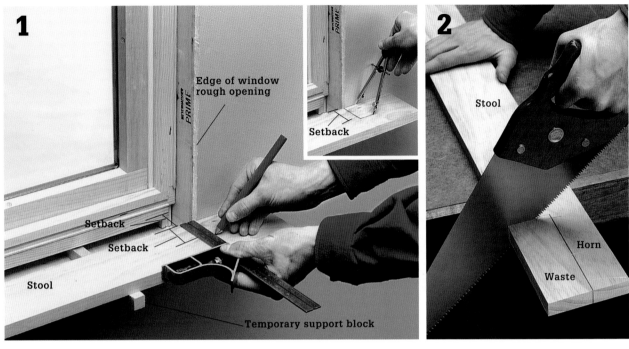

Cut the board for the stool to length, with several extra inches at each end for the horns. Temporarily position the stool in the window opening, pressed against the wall and centered on the window. Use a combination square to measure the setback distance from the window frame to the near edge of the stool. Mark the setback onto the stool at each edge of the window rough opening (if the measurements are different, use the greater setback distance for each end). Then use a compass and pencil to scribe the profile of the wall onto the stool to complete the cutting line for the horn (inset photo).

Cut out the notches to create the stool horns. For straight lines, you can use a large handsaw, but for the scribed line use a more maneuverable saw like the jigsaw or a coping saw. Test-fit the stool, making any minor adjustments with a plane or a rasp so it fits tightly to the window frame and flush against the walls.

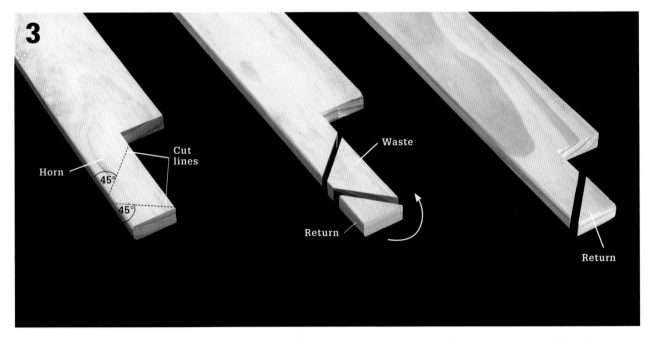

To create a return at the horn of the stool, miter-cut the return pieces at 45° angles. Mark the stool at its overall length and cut it to size with 45° miter cuts. Glue the return to the mitered end of the horn so the grain wraps around the corner. **Note:** Use this same technique to create the returns on the apron, but make the cuts with the apron held on edge, rather than flat.

(continued)

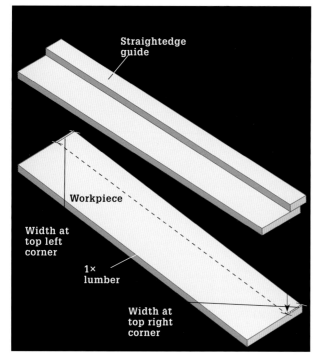

TIP: Where jamb extensions are needed, cut the head extension to its finished length—the distance between the window side jambs plus the thickness of both side extensions (typically 1× stock). For the width, measure the distance between the window jamb and the finished wall at each corner; then mark the measurements on the ends of the extension. Use a straightedge to draw a reference line connecting the points. Build a simple cutting jig, as shown.

Clamp the jig on the reference line, and rip the extension to width. Using a circular saw; keep the baseplate tight against the jig and move the saw smoothly through the board. Reposition the clamp when you near the end of the cut. Cut both side extensions to length and width, using the same technique as for the head extension (see TIP at left).

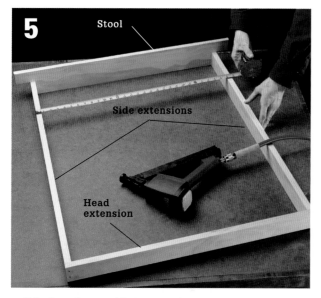

Build a box frame with the extensions and stool, using 6d finish nails and a pneumatic nailer. Measure to make sure the box has the same dimensions as the window jambs. Drive nails through the top of the head extension into the side extensions and through the bottom of the stool into side extensions.

Apply wood glue to the back edge of the frame, and position it against the front edge of the window jambs. Use wood shims to adjust the frame, making sure the pieces are flush with the window jambs. Fasten the frame at each shim location, using 8d finish nails driven through pilot holes. Loosely pack insulation between the studs and the jambs, or use minimal-expanding spray foam.

7

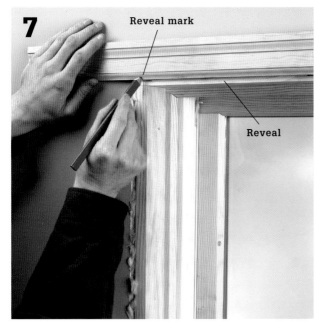

Reveal mark

Reveal

On the edge of each jamb or jamb extension, mark a ³⁄₁₆" to ¼" reveal. Place a length of casing along the head extension, aligned with the reveal marks at the corners. Mark where the reveal marks intersect; then make 45° miter cuts at each point. Reposition the casing at the head extension and attach, using 4d finish nails at the extensions and 6d finish nails at the framing members.

8

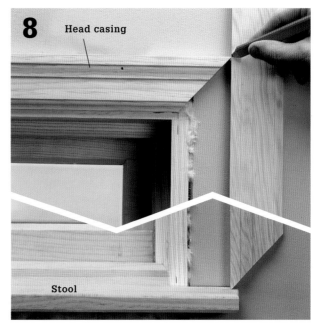

Head casing

Stool

Cut the side casings to rough length, leaving the ends slightly long for final trimming. Miter one end at 45°. With the pointed end on the stool, mark the height of the side casing at the top edge of the head casing.

9

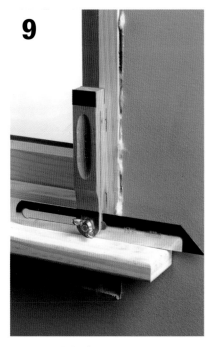

To get a tight fit for side casings, align one side of a T-bevel with the reveal, mark the side extension and position the other side flush against the horn. Transfer the angle from the T-bevel to the end of the casing, and cut the casing to length.

10

Test-fit the casings, making any final adjustments with a plane or rasp. Fasten the casing with 4d finish nails at the extensions and 6d finish nails at the framing members.

11

Cut the apron to length, leaving a few inches at each end for creating the returns (step 3). Position the apron tight against the bottom edge of the stool, and then attach it, using 6d finish nails driven every 12".

Arts & Crafts Casing

Traditional Arts & Crafts casings are made of simple, flat materials with little to no decorative molding trimmed out of the stock. Add nonmitered corners to the mix and this casing becomes as plain as possible. The back band installed on the perimeter of this project is optional, but it adds depth to the window treatment while maintaining a simple style.

Traditionally, the wood used for this style of trim is quartersawn oak. The term "quartersawn" refers to the method of milling the material. Quartersawn oak is easily distinguishable from plain-sawn oak by its tight grain pattern laced with rays of lighter color also known as rifts. Quartersawn oak is more expensive than plain oak and may only be available at lumberyards or hardwood supply stores, depending upon your area. Either plain-sawn or quartersawn oak will fit the style of this casing.

To begin the installation of this trim style, refer to pages 102 and 105 to read the step-by-step process for installing jamb extensions, if necessary, and the stool portion of this project.

Tools & Materials ▸

Tape measure	Combination square
Straightedge	Compass
Power miter saw	Nail set
Circular saw	1 × 4 finish lumber
or jigsaw	Back band trim
Handsaw	Wood shims
Plane or rasp	4d, 6d, and 8d finish
Drill hammer	nails
Pneumatic nailer	Finishing putty
	Eye protection

The Arts & Crafts style is similar to the overall look and feel of Mission furniture, as can be seen in this relatively simple oak window casing.

How to Install Arts & Crafts Casing

Follow the step-by-step process on pages 103 to 105 to install the stool and jamb extensions. Set a combination square to ³⁄₁₆" or ¼" and mark a reveal line on the top and side jambs.

To find the length of the head casing and apron, measure the distance between the reveal lines on the side jambs and add twice the width of the side casings. Cut the head casing and the apron to length. Install the head casing flush with the top reveal line. Use a scrap piece of trim to line up the head casing horizontally.

Measure and cut the side casings to length. Install them flush with the reveal lines. Make sure the joints at the top and bottom are tight. Measure the distance to the end of the stool from the outer edge of the side casing. Install the apron tight to the bottom of the stool at the same dimension from the end of the stool.

Back band

Measure, cut, and install the back band around the perimeter of the window casings, mitering the joints at the corners. Continue the back band around the edge of the apron, mitering the corners. Nail the back band in place with 4d finish nails.

Basement Window Trim

Basement windows bring much-needed sunlight into dark areas, but even in finished basements they often get ignored on the trim front. This is partly because most basement foundation walls are at least 8" thick, often a lot thicker. Add a furred-out wall and the window starts to look more like a tunnel with a pane of glass at the end. But with some well-designed and well-executed trim carpentry, you can turn the depth disadvantage into a positive.

A basement window opening may be finished with drywall, but the easiest way to trim one is by making extrawide custom jambs that extend from the inside face of the window frame to the interior wall surface. Because of the extra width, plywood stock is a good choice for the custom jambs. The project shown here is created with veneer-core plywood with oak veneer surface. The jamb members are fastened together into a nice square frame using rabbet joints at the corner. The frame is scribed and installed as a single unit and then trimmed out with oak casing. The casing is applied flush with the inside edges of the frame opening. If you prefer to have a reveal edge around the interior edge of the casing, you will need to add a solid hardwood strip to the edge of the frame so the plies of the plywood are not visible.

Tools & Materials ▸

Pencil	Clamps
Tape measure	Finish-grade ¾" oak
Tablesaw	plywood
Drill with bits	Spray-foam insulation
2-ft. level	Composite or cedar
Framing square	wood shims
Utility knife	1¼", 2" finish nails
Straightedge	1⅝" drywall screws
Miter saw	Carpenter's glue
Router and	Eye protection
router table	

Because they are set into thick foundation walls, basement windows present a bit of a trimming challenge. But the thickness of the foundation wall also lets you create a handy ledge that's deep enough to hold potted plants or even sunning cats.

How to Trim a Basement Window

Check to make sure the window frame and surrounding area are dry and free of rot, mold, or damage. At all four corners of the basement window, measure from the inside edge of the window frame to the wall surface. Add 1" to the longest of these measurements.

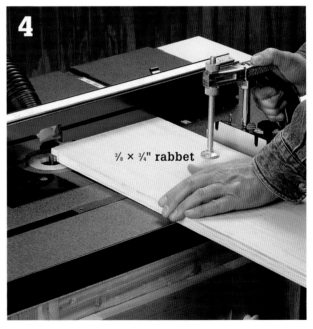

Set your tablesaw to make a rip cut to the width arrived at in step 1. If you don't have a tablesaw, set up a circular saw and straightedge cutting guide to cut strips to this length. With a fine-tooth panel-cutting blade, rip enough plywood strips to make the four jamb frame components.

Miter gauge

Cross-cut the plywood strips to correct lengths. In our case, we designed the jamb frame to be the exact same outside dimensions as the window frame, since there was some space between the jamb frame and the rough opening.

⅜ × ¾" rabbet

Cut ⅜"-deep × ¾"-wide rabbets at each end of the head jamb and the sill jamb. A router table is the best tool for this job, but you may use a tablesaw or handsaws and chisels. Inspect the jambs first and cut the rabbets in whichever face is in better condition. To ensure uniformity, we ganged the two jambs together (they're the same length). It's also a good idea to include backer boards to prevent tearout.

(continued)

5

Glue and clamp the frame parts together, making sure to clamp near each end from both directions. Set a carpenter's square inside the frame and check it to make sure it's square.

6

Before the glue sets, carefully drill three perpendicular pilot holes, countersunk, through the rabbeted workpieces and into the side jambs at each corner. Space the pilot holes evenly, keeping the end ones at least ¾" in from the end. Drive a 1⅝" drywall screw into each pilot hole, taking care not to overdrive. Double check each corner for square as you work, adjusting the clamps if needed.

7

Let the glue dry for at least one hour (overnight is better). Then remove the clamps and set the frame in the window opening. Adjust the frame so it is centered and level in the opening and the exterior-side edges fit flush against the window frame.

8

Taking care not to disturb the frame's position (rest a heavy tool on the sill to hold it in place if you wish), press a steel rule against the wall surface and mark trimming points at the point where the rule meets the jambs at each side of all four frame corners, using a sharp pencil.

Remove the frame and clamp it on a flat work surface. Use a straightedge to connect the scribe marks at the ends of each jamb frame side. Set the cutting depth of your circular saw to just a small fraction over ¾". Clamp a straightedge guide to the frame so the saw blade will follow the cutting line and trim each frame side in succession. (The advantage to using a circular saw here is that any tearout from the blade will be on the nonvisible faces of the frame).

Replace the frame in the window opening in the same orientation as when you scribed it and install shims until it is level and centered in the opening. Drive a few finish nails (hand or pneumatic) through the side jambs into the rough frame. Also drive a few nails through the sill jamb. Most trim carpenters do not drive nails into the head jamb.

Insulate between the jamb frame and the rough frame with spray-in polyurethane foam. Look for minimal-expanding foam labeled "window and door" and don't spray in too much. Let the foam dry for a half hour or so and then trim off the excess with a utility knife. TIP: Protect the wood surfaces near the edges with wide strips of masking tape.

Remove the masking tape and clean up the mess from the foam (there is always some). Install case molding. We used picture-frame techniques to install fairly simple oak casing.

Decorative Door Header

Adding a decorative head casing to a door is a simple way to dress up your existing trim. Although head treatments are more common over doors, this project will work for window trim as well. Designing your own decorative molding can be creative and fun, but try not to overwhelm the room with an elaborate piece, or it may detract from the décor.

Standard stock door casings have an outer-edge thickness of approximately $^{11}\!/_{16}"$. Build your custom header around this thickness. Use it to create a reveal line to a thinner piece of trim, or build out from the edge for a bolder, more substantial appearance. In the project shown, a bed molding, or smaller piece of crown molding, is used to build out the header away from the wall. The ends of the molding are returned to the wall, and the entire piece is capped with a piece of lattice molding. Installing a decorative header of this style on an interior door may require the installation of additional blocking. For installation over an exterior door or a window, nail the pieces in place directly to the load-bearing framing in the wall above the opening.

Tools & Materials ▶

Pencil
Tape measure
Power miter saw
Finish nail gun

Brad nail gun
Moldings
Wood glue
Eye protection

Replacing plain head casing on a door or window with a decorative built-up version is a quick and easy way to add some sophistication to any ordinary feature of your home.

How to Install a Decorative Door Header

Measure the width of your door casing and rough-cut a piece of bed or crown molding 6" longer. Use the casing width dimension to layout cut marks on the bottom edge of the molding. Start the marks 2" from the end to allow space for cutting the mitered ends.

With the molding upside down and sprung against the fence, cut a 45° outside corner miter angle at each end, on the casing reference marks from step 1.

Cut mitered returns for the molding using the leftover piece. Set the angle of the power miter saw to the opposing 45° angle and cut the returns with the molding upside down and sprung against the fence. Dry-fit the pieces, recutting them if necessary. Apply glue to the return pieces and nail them to the ends of the head molding with 1" brad nails.

Nail the new header in place with 2½" finish nails driven at an angle through the bed molding and into the framing members of the wall.

Cut lattice molding 1" longer than the length of the bed molding and nail it in place with ⅝" brad nails so that it has a uniform overhang of ½" Fill all nail holes with spackle and sand them with fine-grit sandpaper. Apply the final coat of finish.

Wall Opening

Trimming out a drywall opening is an easy way to add style to any room transition using decorative trim. Although this project may be done with paint-grade materials, clear finish adds detail and inviting wood grain, showcasing the opening.

In the project shown, solid wood trim is used to cover the drywall jambs of the opening. This technique can also be accomplished with plywood jambs. However, to maintain a constant reveal with the rest of the room, a thin strip of solid oak material should be applied to the edges of the plywood to cover the visible plies. This application should be done prior to installing the jambs to avoid fastening difficulties.

The odds are good that the finished drywall corners are irregular, causing some minor differences in wall thickness along the jambs of the opening. When these irregularities are minor, (less than ³⁄₁₆"), it is best to cut the jamb material at the widest jamb measurement and let the casing bridge the difference. When wall thickness varies a lot (³⁄₁₆" or more), it is better to cut tapered jambs to cover the difference.

Tools & Materials ▸

Pry bar	Framing square
Side cutters	Jamb material (lumber
Pencil	or plywood)
Tape measure	Case moldings
Circular saw and	Base moldings
straightedge guide	2½" finish nails
4-ft. level	Wood glue
Pneumatic finish	Shims
nail gun	Scrap 2 × 4 material
Power miter saw	

Before

Passthrough openings between rooms often are left very plain by the builders, especially in more modern homes. Not only is this a dull design statement; it also exposes the edges of the drywall openings to damage. A little bit of door casing and new jambs can bring new life to the opening (and protect it as well).

How to Trim a Wall Opening

Remove the existing base molding with a pry bar and hammer. Be careful not to mar the surface of the moldings as you remove them. Pull the nails out of the moldings through the back face with an end nippers or side cutters.

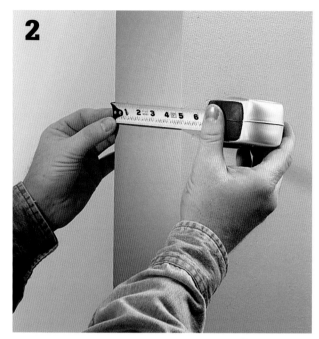

Measure the width and length of the head jamb and the width of each side jamb. Measure each jamb at both ends as well as in the middle of each run. Take note of the measurements. If a jamb differs in width by more than ³⁄₁₆", install a tapered length (see TIP, below).

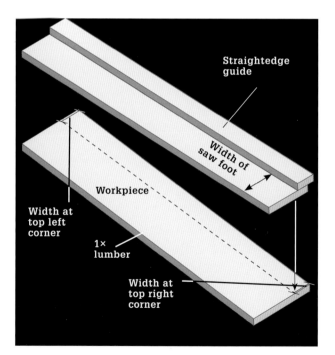

Straightedge guide

Width of saw foot

Workpiece

Width at top left corner

1× lumber

Width at top right corner

TIP: Jambs that do not taper can be cut on a tablesaw, but if you have enough variation in your jamb widths that a taper is called for, make a simple cutting jig and taper-cut the jambs to width with a circular saw. Then lay out the dimensions on the head jamb using the measurements from step 2. The head jamb should run the full length of the opening

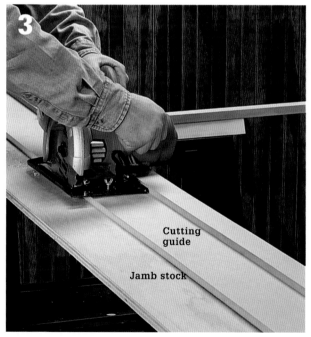

Cutting guide

Jamb stock

Clamp a straightedge guide (TIP, left) to the head jamb on the reference line from the measurements of step 2, and cut the piece to width with a circular saw. Keep the base plate tight against the fence and move the saw smoothly through the board. Reposition the clamp when you near the end of the board.

(continued)

Position the head jamb at the top of the opening, flush with the edges, and nail it in place starting in the middle. Before nailing the ends of the head jamb, check it for square with the walls of the opening, adjusting with shims if necessary. Drive a pair of 2" finish nails every 16".

Place a T-bevel on the floor at the bottom of each side jamb to check for any angled cuts necessary to follow the pitch of the floor. The handle of the bevel should rest against the outer face of the wall, with the blade across the floor.

Transfer the angle from the T-bevel in step 5 to a power miter saw and cut the side jambs to length. The top end of the jamb should be cut square (90°). Each jamb should butt against the head jamb and fit tightly to the finished flooring.

7

Nail the side jambs in place using pairs of 2" finish nails driven every 16" along the jamb. Check the edges of the jamb pieces as you go to make sure they are flush with the surface of the wall.

8

Install casing around the opening. Maintain a consistent ³⁄₁₆" to ¼" reveal around the opening.

9

Measure, cut, and reinstall the existing baseboard so that the ends butt into the sides of the casing. Cut and reinstall the base shoe using mitered or beveled returns (page 59).

10

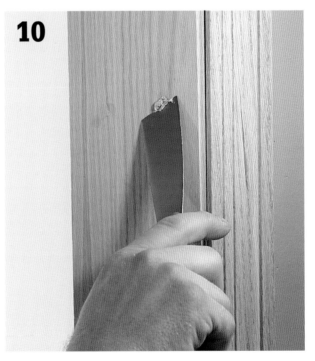

Fill all nail holes with finishing putty and apply a final coat of polyurethane or your finish of choice (try to match existing trim in the room).

Wall Frame Moldings

Adding wall frame moldings is a traditional decorative technique used to highlight special features of a room, divide large walls into smaller sections, or simply add interest to plain surfaces. You can paint the molding the same color as the walls or use a contrasting color. For even greater contrast, paint or wallcover the areas within the frames.

Decorative wood moldings with curved contours work best for wall frames. Chair rail, picture rail, base shoe, cove, quarter-round, and other suitable molding types in several wood species are readily available at home centers and lumberyards.

To determine the sizes and locations of the frames, cut strips of paper to the width of the molding and tape them to the wall. You may want the frames to match the dimensions of architectural details in the room, such as windows or a fireplace.

Install the molding with small finish nails driven at each wall stud location and at the ends of the pieces. Use nails long enough to penetrate the studs by ¾". If there aren't studs where you need them, secure the molding with dabs of construction adhesive.

Tools & Materials ▶

Level	Tape
Framing square	Wood finishing
Miter box and	materials
backsaw	Construction adhesive
Drill and bits	Paintable latex caulk or
Nail set	wood putty
Paper strips	Eye protection

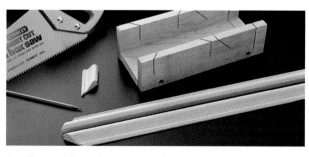

Cut the molding pieces to length, using a miter box and a backsaw (or power miter saw) to cut the ends at 45°. The top and bottom pieces should be the same length, as should the side pieces. Test-fit the pieces, and make any necessary adjustments.

Wall frame moldings use ordinary trim pieces to create frames with mitered corners that give the illusion of frame-and-panel construction.

How to Install Wall Frame Moldings

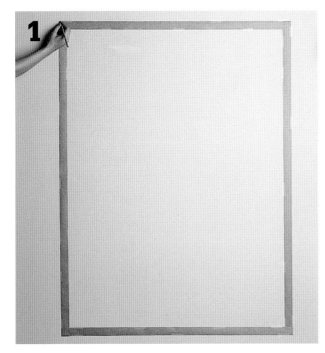

Cut paper strips to the width of the molding, and tape them to the wall. Use a framing square and level to make sure the frame is level and the strips are square to one another. Mark the outer corners of the frame with light pencil lines.

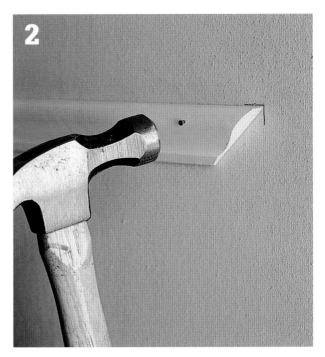

Paint or stain the moldings as desired. Position the top molding piece on the placement marks and tack it in place with two finish nails. If necessary, drill pilot holes for the nails to prevent splitting.

Tack the side moldings in place, using the framing square to make sure they are square to the top piece. Tack up the bottom piece. Adjust the frame, if necessary, so that all of the joints fit tightly, and then completely fasten the pieces.

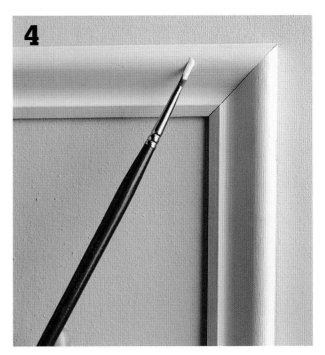

Drive the nails slightly below the surface, using a nail set. Fill the nail holes (and corner joints, if necessary) with wood putty. Touch up the patched areas with paint or stain.

Wainscot Frames

Frame-and-panel wainscot adds depth, character, and a sense of old-world charm to any room. Classic wainscot was built with grooved or rabbeted rails and stiles that captured a floating hardwood panel. In the project shown here, the classic appearance is mimicked, but the difficulties of machining precise parts and commanding craftsman-level joinery are eliminated. Paint-grade materials (mostly MDF) are used in the project shown; however, you can also build the project with solid hardwoods and finish-grade plywood if you prefer a clear-coat finish.

Installing wainscot frames that look like frame-and-panel wainscot can be done piece by piece, but it is often easier to assemble the main frame parts in your shop. Not only does working in the shop allow you to join the frame parts together (we use pocket screws driven in the backs of the rails and stiles); it generally results in a more professional look.

Once the main frames are assembled, they can be attached to the wall at stud locations. If you prefer to site-build the wainscot piece by piece, you may need to replace the wallcovering material with plywood to create nailing surfaces for the individual pieces.

We primed all of the wainscot parts prior to installing them and then painted the wainscot (including the wall sections within the wainscot panel frames) a contrasting color from the wall above the wainscot cap.

Tools & Materials ▶

Laser level
Pencil
Tape measure
Circular saw or tablesaw
Straightedge guide
Power miter saw
Drill with bits
Carpenter's square
Pocket hole jig with screws
Pry bar
Hammer

Pneumatic finish nail gun with compressor
Caulking gun
¾"-thick MDF sheet stock
¹¹⁄₁₆" cove molding
½ × ¾" base shoe
⁹⁄₁₆ × 1⅛" cap molding (10 ft. per panel)
Panel adhesive
Paint and primer
Eye protection

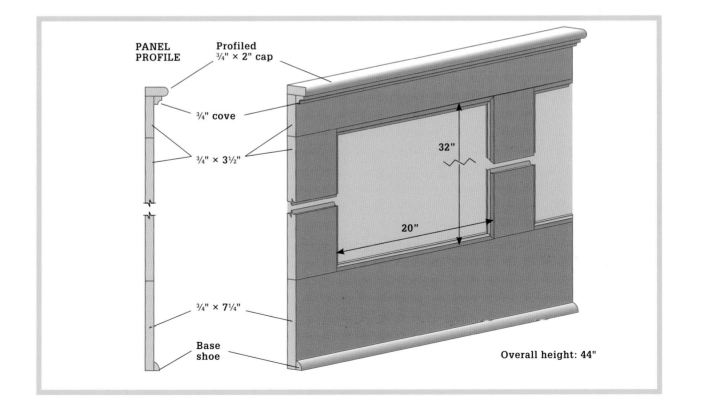

PANEL PROFILE

Profiled ¾" × 2" cap

¾" cove

¾" × 3½"

¾" × 7¼"

Base shoe

32"

20"

Overall height: 44"

How to Install Wainscot Frames

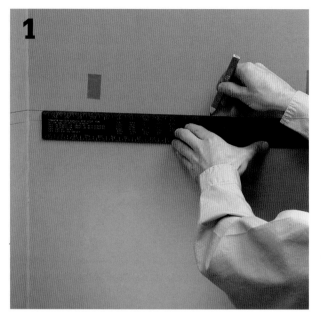

Use a laser level and a pencil to mark the height of the wainscot installation directly onto all walls in the project area. Also mark the height of the top rail (¾" below the overall height), since the cap rail will be installed after the rest of the wainscot is installed. Mark stud locations, using an electronic stud finder.

Plot out the wainscot layout on paper and then test the layout by drawing lines on the wall to make sure you're happy with the design. Try to use a panel width that can be divided evenly into all project wall lengths. In some cases, you may need to make the panel widths slightly different from wall to wall, but make sure to maintain a consistent width within each wall's run.

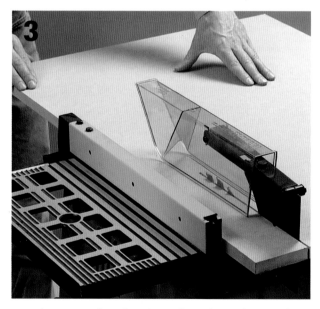

Based on your plan, rip a sheet of MDF into strips to make all of the wainscot parts except the trim moldings. In our case, that included the cap rail (2" wide), the top rail and stiles (3½" wide), and the base rail (7¼" wide). **NOTE:** These are standard lumber dimensions. You can use 1 × 4 and 1 × 4 dimensional lumber for the rails and stiles (use 1 × 2 or rip stock for the cap rail).

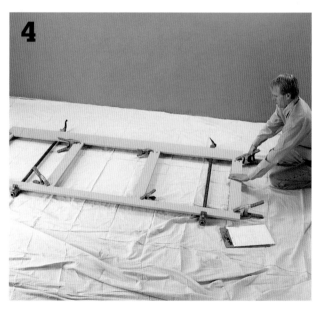

Cut top rails, base rails, and stiles (but not cap rails) to length and dry-assemble the parts into ladder frames based on your layout. Plan the layouts so wall sections longer than 8 ft. are cut with scarf joints in the rails meeting at a stud location. Dry-assemble the pieces on a flat work surface.

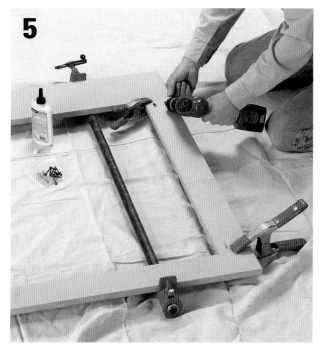

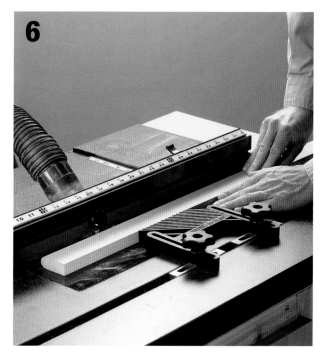

Assemble the frames using glue and pocket screws or biscuits. Clamp the parts together first and check with a carpenter's square to make sure the stiles are perpendicular to both rails.

Mount a ¾" roundover bit in your router or router table and shape a bullnose profile on the front edge of your cap rail stock.

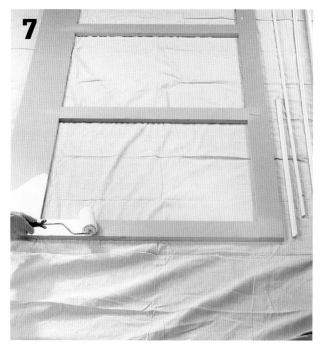

Prime all parts on both sides, including the milled moldings and uncut cap rail stock.

Position the frames against the wall and shim underneath the bottom rails as necessary to bring them flush with the top rail marks on the wall (¾" below the overall height lines). Attach the wainscot sections by driving 3" drywall screws, countersunk, through the top rail and the bottom rail at each stud location. If you are using scarf joints, be sure to install the open half first.

(continued)

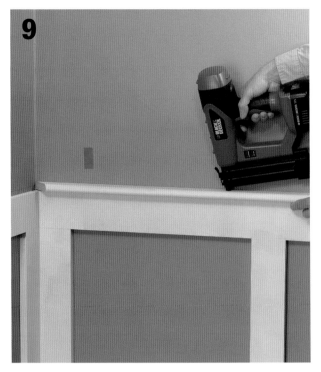

Cut the cap rail to length and attach it to the top rail with panel adhesive and finish nails. Drive a 3" drywall screw through the cap rail and into the wall toenails style at each location. Be sure to carefully drill pilot holes and countersink holes for each screw. Miter-cut the cap rails at the corners.

Install cove molding in the crotch where the cap rail and top rails meet, using glue and a brad nailer. Then nail base shoe to conceal any gaps between the bottoms, rails, and the floor. Miter all corners.

Cut mitered frames to fit around the perimeter of each panel frame created by the rails and stiles. Use cap molding.

Mask the wall above the cap rail and then prime and paint the wainscot frames. Generally, a lighter, contrasting color than the wall color above is most effective visually.

Variation: Natural Wood Finish

1

Snap a level line at the top rail height. Because the rails and stiles are the same thickness, the backer panel should run all the way from the floor to just shy of the top of the top rail. Cut the backers so the grain will run vertically when installed. Attach them to the walls with panel adhesive, notching to fit around obstructions such as this window opening.

2

Install the baseboard and top rail directly over the backer panels, using a finish nailer or by hand-nailing with 6d finish nails. The top edge of the top rail pieces should be slightly higher then the backer panels. Use your reference line as a guide for the top rail, but double check with a level.

3

Attach the cap rail pieces with a finish nailer. The caps should butt flush against the wall, concealing the top edges of the backer panels. Also butt the cap rails against the window and door casings.

4

Cut the stiles to fit between the top rail and the baseboard and install them. It's okay to vary the spacing slightly from wall to wall, but try to keep them evenly spaced on each wall. Where the wainscot meets door or window casing, butt the edges of the stiles against the casing. This can mean notching around window aprons or horns as well as door plinth blocks.

5

Add decorative touches, such as the corbels we cut for this installation. The corbels provide some support for the cap rail but their function is primarily decorative. We glued and nailed one corbel at each end of each cap rail piece and above each stile, and then added an intermediate one between each pair of stiles.

Raised-Panel Wainscot

By definition, wainscot is a treatment to the lower half of a wall. Designs can range from simple architecturally applied moldings directly to the drywall to elaborate rail and style construction with raised-panel centers. Aside from the traditional look of raised-paneled wainscot, these raised panels can be installed on any part of a wall; the lower third, the full wall, or the ceiling.

Tools & Materials ▸

Circular saw
Framing square
Measuring tape
Clamps

Raised-panel
router bit
Recessed router
Eye protection

Raised-Panel Bits ▸

Raised-panel router bits generally require a router table with a powerful ½"-collet router or a shaper to run them successfully. The bit cuts the edge profile into the panel inserts. If you are making traditional raised-panel frames, you'll also need a sticking bit set to cut the edge profiles for the frame rails and stiles.

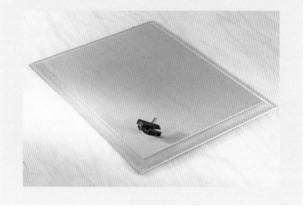

Genuine raised-panel wainscot has depth and substance that can be mimicked with trim moldings, but never duplicated.

How to Install Raised-Panel Wainscot

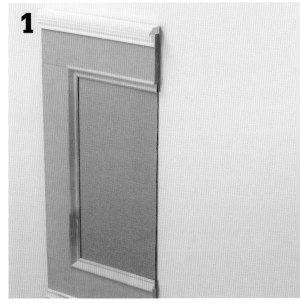

1

Plan your layout and make a mock-up of the wall treatment, including base molding, shoe molding (if you'll use it), lower rail, panel insert, upper rail, bolection moldings and cap moldings.

2

Cut the panel inserts, making sure they are square. If you have access to a tablesaw or a panel-cutting saw, use it. If the panel has a finish-grade side, make sure the blade is cutting down into the finished side to limit any tearout to the back surface. Allow for ¼" clearance between the panels and the frames.

3

Cut the panel edge profiles. After all the raised panels are cut to the proper size, install a panel cutting bit in your router table and cut the edge profiles. One great way to accomplish this is to attach a series of thin auxiliary fences to your router table fence. After making one pass on each side of all the panels, remove one of the sacrificial pieces of MDF to expose more of the panel bit and make another pass. This process is repeated until the full profile has been cut. When complete, you will have a perfectly profiled raised panel.

(continued)

4

Make and install frames for the panels. Here, ¾" thick MDF is ripped into 4"-wide strips and formed into frames that are mounted on the room walls. See pages 120 to 124 for more information on making and installing wainscot frames.

5

Cut ¼"-wide spacers from thin stock—about the same thickness as the edges of the panel inserts. Tack the spacers around the edges of the panel openings in the frame—use at least two spacers at each edge. You can use double-sided tape to hold the spacers, but hot-glue from a hot-glue gun is a better choice.

6

Insert raised panels into openings so the panels fit inside the spacers. Test the fit and make any adjustments as needed.

7

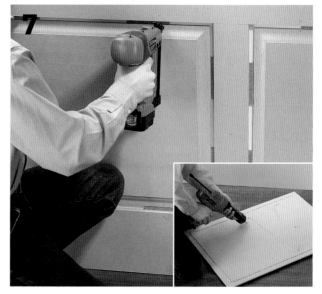

Fasten the raised panels in the frame openings. Use small (18-gauge) pneumatic brads to secure the panels, preferably driven close enough to the edges that the bolection molding will cover the nailheads. **OPTION:** Apply panel adhesive to the back of the panel (inset) before tacking it in place. The adhesive will greatly improve the holding power of the bond, but it also complicates removal of the panels if you need to make an adjustment at some point.

8

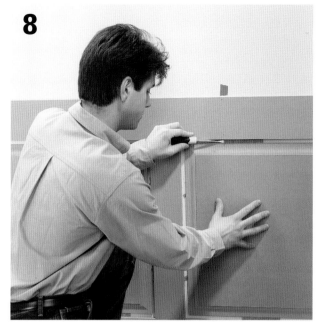

Remove the panel spacers and the top and sides of the opening, prying them loose with a flat screwdriver. Leave the bottom spacers in place as an auxiliary support for the panel, which is fairly heavy.

9

Install base molding according to your trim plan and mock up. Miter or cope the molding at inside corners and miter it at outside corners. Use panel adhesive and pneumatic nails (16-gauge) or 2½"-finish nails to secure the moldings, driving nails at stud locations where possible. Attach base shoe molding if you plan to use it, making sure to fasten it to the base molding and not to the floor.

10

Miter-cut the corners and fasten bolection molding to cover the gaps between the raised panels and the frames. Use high-tack wood trim glue and pneumatic brad nails to attach the bolection molding. Bolection molding (inset) resembles cap molding but is intended to cover gaps and create a shadow line because it stands out from the surfaces to which it is attached.

11

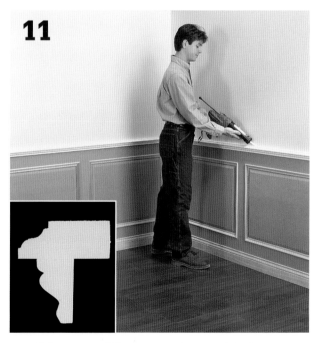

Install the cap molding to cover the tops of the frames, using finish nails or pneumatic nails. Fill nail holes with putty throughout the project and prepare for finishing by sanding lightly and by filling the gap between the cap molding and the wall with a thin bead of paintable caulk. Apply your finish of choice. We used primer and paint, since MDF is not suited for clear finishing.

Jointless Rail-and-Stile Wainscot

Some forces of nature that affect carpentry cannot be avoided, but they can be controlled. One is the natural movement of wood that occurs from changes in temperature and humidity. Many a trim job that is perfect when it is installed in the summer suffers from opened miters and other signs of shrinkage when the humidity drops during the fall and winter heating seasons.

By creating a layout and cutting out panels from a 4 × 8-ft. sheet of MDF, you can control the number of joints and greatly reduce the affects of wood movement. MDF is a manmade material composed of sawdust and resins and formed without a grain pattern under extremely high pressure, which makes it one of the most dimensionally stable wood products. Although all materials will be affected somewhat by humidity changes, MDF is affected the least.

After careful planning and measuring, the design and layout of the room can be transferred directly to a story pole stick. This can be transferred to the 4 × 8 sheet so layouts can be consistent. After cutting out the center panel, the remaining material becomes the rails and stiles. The panel itself is squared up and run through a router bit, creating the raised panel. Bolection molding is then cut and used to trim out each panel.

Tools & Materials ▸

Circular saw	Clamps
Cutting guide	Jigsaw
Measuring tape	MDF
	Eye protection

These wainscot frames are cut from full sheets of MDF, so they require virtually no joinery.

How to Install Jointless Wainscot

Plan your layout. Measure the length of each wainscot run and calculate a plan that minimizes the number of vertical joints. The goal is to have all of the panel inserts the same width. Do not have panels meet in vertical joints in the stile areas. Butt the "rails" against a full-width stile in the adjoining panel.

Mark a layout line on the wall at the planned wainscot height. Generally, 36" to 42" is the typical height range, although on older homes, full-height or nearly full-wall height wainscot coverage was not uncommon. Use a laser level to mark the height if you have access to one.

Lay out the cutting lines on your MDF panels, following your plan. For uniform results, create and use a layout stick to mark the locations of the margins and panel widths.

Set up for the panel cutouts. To get the straightest possible line when removing the panel from the frame material, use a circular saw and a straightedge cutting guide. Clamp the guide to the panel so the saw foot setback has the blade falling just inside the layout line. Set the saw cutting depth to about ⅛" deeper than the thickness of the stock (⅞" for ¾" MDF panels).

(continued)

5

Make a plunge cut. Position the saw so the blade will come down well within the start of the waste area. Press the foot firmly against the straightedge guide. Hold the saw so the blade is slightly above the work surface. Turn on the saw. Once the blade is rotating at full speed, carefully lower the saw onto the workpiece, holding onto the handle with a firm grip. This is called a plunge cut. Without pressing down too hard and forcing the blade, let the blade cut into and through the workpiece.

6

Set up for the panel cutouts following the straightedge guide. Be careful, but don't proceed too slowly or the blade may cause some burning. Stop cutting an inch or so before the blade reaches the cutting line. Make all internal plunge cuts on all frame sections.

7

Finish the cutouts with a jigsaw. Make sure the workpiece and the waste are well supported from below, and use a jigsaw to compete the cutouts at the corners.

8

Sand the corner smooth with a detail sander or a random orbit sander. Hand sanding is also an option.

Ogee bit with bead

OPTION: Cut a decorative edge profile on the frame cutouts using a router and a piloted profiling bit, such as the ogee bit seen here (inset). Exercise some care, particularly around the corners. If you are planning to shape and install insert panels, you generally should not profile the frame, too.

9

Prime and paint the frames. Use a small brush to paint the profiled areas and use a small roller sleeve to coat the rail and stile areas. Also paint the cap molding and base trim with a small paint roller.

10

Prepare the walls. You have many design options here. The simplest is to paint the wall the same color as the wainscot frames. Or, you can paint it a contrasting color. By using a paintable, embossed wallpaper you can add some interesting texture. Or you can apply natural wood paneling, mirrored glass panels—there is virtually no limit to the possibilities.

11

Install the frame with panel adhesive and pneumatic nails or 8d finish nails driven at stud locations. Cut biscuit slots at the stile-and-rail joints and use biscuits to assist in the alignment. Add base and cap molding as desired.

Working with Bolection Molding

The molding used to trim around raised-panel wainscot is called bolection molding. This molding has a rabbet cut on the inside that allows it to span from the rails and stiles to the edges of the raised panel. In order to cut this molding properly and accurately, a jig has to be used. A sacrificial piece of MDF is clamped to the saw. The position of this fence is set by using a piece of the bolection molding. One edge of the bolection molding sits on the edge of the sacrificial clamped fence and the other just touches the vertical fence. This will allow the molding to rest securely in position. By using this sacrificial fence you will be able to cut bolection molding safely and accurately.

Tools & Materials ▸

Chop Saw
Saw helper fence
Measuring tape
Clamps

Sacrificial material at
  least 36"
Eye protection

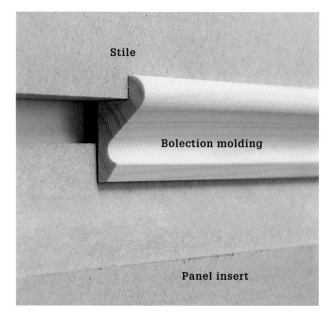

Bolection molding is designed to cover the gap between the panel insert and the frame in a frame-and-panel construction. In trim carpentry, this type of assembly is found most often in wainscot.

How to Miter-cut Bolection Molding

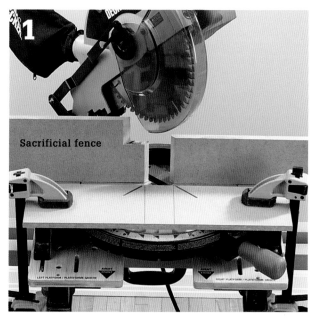

Set up your power miter saw for the cuts. Clamp or screw pieces of MDF to both sides of the saw fence to make sacrificial fences. Clamp another piece of MDF to the saw table so you can make alignment cuts.

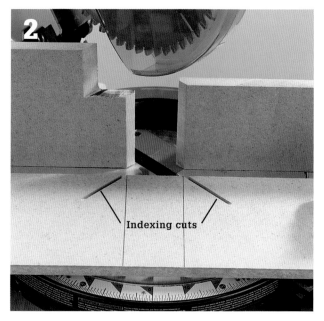

Make indexing cuts. To establish where the blade will land, make two 45° cuts in the sacrificial fence. Because you have clamped a sacrificial table to the saw table, the blade will create horizontal indexing cuts as well. On the table, draw reference lines straight out from the outside edge of each indexing cut in the fence.

Mark molding for a miter cut. Because of the profile of the bolection molding, the inside edge of the molding where it needs to be mitered is not even with the very edge of the molding. The actual cutting line should be about ⅜" in from the end. Make the miter cut.

Mark the other end of the workpiece for cutting. To measure the other end of the piece, align the mark made in step 3 with the edge of the saw table and make your measurement starting at the table edge. Make the miter cut.

Mark the opposing miter. Align the measure cutting line from step 4 with the perpendicular indexing line on the sacrificial table.

Make the opposing miter cut with the power miter saw and test the joint between moldings to make sure it is square.

Ceiling Medallions

A ceiling medallion is an elegant style accent that can highlight a light fixture or establish the visual focal point of a room all on its own. Most medallions today are made of polyurethane and are available at home centers off the shelf in various styles and sizes. Specialty restoration dealers carry extensive lines of medallions as well.

In the project shown, a medallion is installed over a light fixture. Depending on the style of medallion you choose, a hole may need to be cut in the center to allow access to the electrical mechanicals in the ceiling. If you are installing the medallion over a light fixture, turn off the power at the main service panel before you begin.

Tools & Materials ▸

Screwdriver
Adjustable wrench
Pencil
Drill with bits and
   circle cutter
Caulk gun

Medallion
150-grit sandpaper
Polyurethane adhesive
Threaded nipple
Wallboard screws
Paintable latex caulk

Ceiling medallions are classic trim accessories, and most sold today are designed to be installed in conjunction with a ceiling light fixture. Some medallions come as solid discs (carved wood, cast plaster, or more commonly, urethane) and others are two-piece assemblies that can be slipped between the light and the ceiling and snapped together.

How to Install a Ceiling Medallion

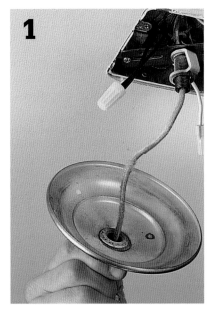

1

Turn the power off at the main service panel. Remove the cover plate of the light fixture. Disconnect the fixture wires, taking note of the color of the wires of each connection. If necessary, unscrew the supporting nipple in the center of the electrical box and set the fixture aside.

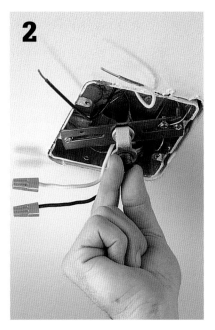

2

Compensate for the added thickness of the medallion by adding a longer nipple to the center of the electrical box. If a nipple is not used, purchase longer screws to reattach the cover plate to the mounting strap once the medallion is installed.

3

Cut a hole in the center of the medallion using a circle cutter and a drill. The hole should be smaller than the cover plate, but large enough to access the screw holes on the mounting strap. Lightly sand the back of the medallion with 150-grit sandpaper.

4

Position the medallion on the ceiling centered over the electrical box. Trace the outline with a pencil. Apply adhesive to the back of the medallion, staying 1" away from the outer edge. Align the medallion with the pencil line and press it to the ceiling.

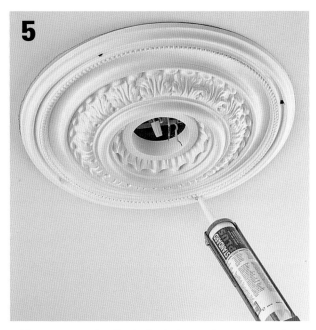

5

Drill countersunk pilot holes in inconspicuous areas of the medallion and drive drywall screws through the holes to hold it in place until the adhesive dries. Fill the holes with paintable latex caulk, smoothing the holes with a wet finger. Paint the medallion as desired, and reattach the light when the paint is completely dry.

Coffered Ceilings

Installing a coffered ceiling is one of the most lavish treatments you can perform on a ceiling. It adds both beauty and character and is a great way to cultivate a more formal atmosphere in a room. Coffered ceilings, sometimes referred to as box beams, consist of recessed panels or individual cells of intersecting beams that are trimmed with moldings.

These individual cells can either be squares or rectangles: the precise shape is dictated by the layout of the room they are being installed in. The types of moldings used, the depth of the individual cells, and the reveals can all change the look of the coffer to make it resemble a particular style, such as Craftsman, Federal, or Victorian. Creating a coffer depth too big in a smaller room can be overwhelming. Taller ceilings (above 9 ft.) should have deeper cells of around 5" to 8", while a traditional 8 to 9-ft. ceiling would have a depth anywhere from 2" to 5".

The method that is shown in this chapter will create the illusion that heavy solid beams were used, but in fact simple, lightweight three-sided hollow boxes are all you need. Once the boxes are installed to the ceiling, planks of MDF are used to complete the box. When affixing these to the ceiling, plenty of good quality construction adhesive is used, along with nailing securely into joists wherever possible.

Tools & Materials ▸

¾" MDF panels	Finish nailer
1 × 6 pine	16g (or 8d) finish
5" base molding	nails
4⅝" crown molding	Carpenters square
Power miter saw	Glue/construction
Measuring tape	adhesive
#2.5 pencil	Eye protection

The rich architectural appeal of a coffered ceiling can be achieved with some strips of MDF and a little crown molding.

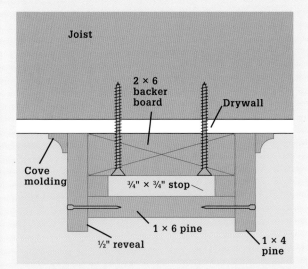

Exposed beams lend a feeling of strength and structure to a room, even if they're really just hollow shells like the beams seen here. Because they can be attached directly to the ceiling surface, installing decorative beams is a relatively easy trim carpentry project (as long as you're comfortable working at heights).

A cross section view of the exposed beams shown being installed here reveals that they are hollow inside and actually quite simple in structure. You can install beams in any direction, but perpendicular to the ceiling joists (as shown above) is the easier orientation to work with.

How to Install a Coffered Ceiling

Take measurements and plan your layout. Divide the ceiling into square or rectangular sections that are proportional to the overall size. The general idea is to install series of plus-shape nailers to establish each point of intersection, and then connect the nailers with strips of MDF.

Mark the layout lines for the ceiling and snap chalk lines to establish the grid you'll be basing your layout on.

(continued)

3

Construct the three-sided boxes that will create the nailer unions that define each coffered section. The boxes are made from 1 x 6 pine.

4

Hang the nailer union assemblies from the ceiling according to your layout plans. Use deck screws driven up through the boxes and into ceiling joists where possible. If no joists are available in the installation area, use toggle bolts.

5

Hang T-shaped nailer union assemblies next to the walls according to your installation plan.

.

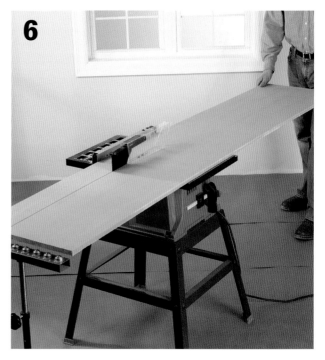

6

Cut strips of MDF to make the beam covers. Allow an extra 1½" of width so the beam covers will conceal the bottom edges of the beam sides after they are installed. Also rip the stock for the beam sides (this should be equal in width to the depth of the nailer boxes).

7

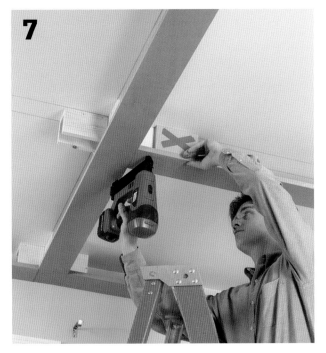

Attach the MDF strips to the bottoms of the nailers and then to the sides, using panel adhesive and 16-gauge pneumatic finish nails. Then install the beam side strips, making adjustments as needed to ensure that the surfaces of the sides are flush with the edges of the beam covers.

8

Measure the inside dimensions of each coffer so you can make a crown molding frame that is preassembled on the ground and then simply lifted up into place and secured.

9

Cut crown molding and assemble it into a square frame on the ground. Short each dimension by about 1⁄32" to make sure the frame will fit inside. You'll have the best chance for success if you measure and build each frame individually.

10

Lift the finished crown molding frames up into the coffer opening and secure with pneumatic finish nails. Caulk all gaps, fill nail holes, and then paint and prime. Add ceiling medallion and other ornamental millwork if you wish, but use discretion.

Custom Moldings

Creating your own custom trim moldings can be a simple and rewarding process if you own the right tools and start out with proper materials. Nothing looks better than a room with one-of-a-kind trim, and your pride in knowing that you didn't just install the trim, but actually created it yourself will stay with you forever. Beyond the satisfaction of knowing that you did it yourself, you may be asking why anyone would make custom trim work.

The most common reason to create your own trim is to match the existing moldings of your home. The moldings of older homes are more unusual and in some cases were milled by hand, making it difficult to match the profiles with any of today's stock materials. If the trim from a remodeling project is not salvageable, you may find a need for just a few lineal feet of matching material. Short runs of specialized trim components from professional mill shops are expensive and not cost effective.

Another reason to create your own moldings is to match an existing species of wood in your home. Stock moldings are generally available in a few commonly used materials, leaving out species such as walnut, cherry, ash, or hickory. If the hardwood floor of your formal dining room is hickory, finding matching casings for the windows and doors will be nearly impossible—unless you do it yourself.

No matter the reason, creating your own moldings requires patience and proper materials. Using machinery to create trim that is uniform from the first foot to the last can be challenging. Router settings must be precise, and bits must be sharp. Whenever possible, machine each piece of trim you need plus a few extra to make up for bad cuts and blemishes in the material.

Material preparation is the most important part of creating uniform custom moldings. "Blank" stock that will be turned into moldings needs to be machined squarely and at a uniform thickness with a planer, jointer, and a tablesaw. Inaccurate thicknesses and material that differs in width will show up at every joint of the installation. If you do not have access to this machinery, consider asking a small cabinet shop in your area to provide the service for you. Finish-sand each piece of material prior to molding it. This will avoid excess chatter marks and unnecessary sanding, which could remove the profile you mold.

A router and profiling bit can convert just about any piece of wood stock into a trim board. Generally, it works best to cut the profile with your router and then rip the workpiece to finished width on your tablesaw.

Router Tables

Router tables add a considerable amount of versatility to routing. With the tool secured below the table and the bit exposed above, you can use both hands to run the workpiece past the bit, often without hold-downs or special clamping. The fence provides the means for controlling the cut, just like a tablesaw fence. Together with the flat, stable surface of the tabletop, the fence allows safe, accurate cuts with quick setups. Using a bearing-guided bit, you can rout without the fence, using the table for support. A basic shop-made version can be inexpensive and easy to build, and may be all you need. Or you can buy one of the many commercial tables available.

As a general rule, router bits with a diameter over 1¾" are much safer to use in a router table. Big bits can be hard to control with handheld routers, especially on edge-forming operations. When using large bits with the router table, cover as much of the bit as possible with the fence and cut incrementally with light passes. Make sure to adjust the speed of the router when possible, according to the bit manufacturer's specifications. Many large bits are designed for use in a table only.

Commercial tables are available as clamp-on tabletop, benchtop, and floor models. In terms of quality, the overall field runs wide, as does the price range.

When shopping, look closely at the main components—the tabletop, the fence, and the base—and compare the usability features such as fence adjustments and overall versatility. There are many great tables to choose from with quality safety features.

Shop-made router tables can be every bit as advanced as commercial units when you purchase specific components through a woodworking store or supply catalog. Often, shop-made units are a better option because they allow you to adjust the table size to suit the type of routing you most frequently do. Purchasing the individual components of your router table also allows you to customize each piece with the options you want, rather than getting a complete package.

Understand proper feed directions and techniques before you begin using a table router. Unlike handheld operations where the material is clamped down, with a router table the workpiece moves freely, creating the possibility off kickbacks and other dangerous situations. Read all manufacturer's warnings and techniques before you begin.

A shop-made router table is built from parts available at woodworking stores and catalogs. A variable speed control dial with on/off switch, as well as a fence with integrated dust collection, are just a few of the available options.

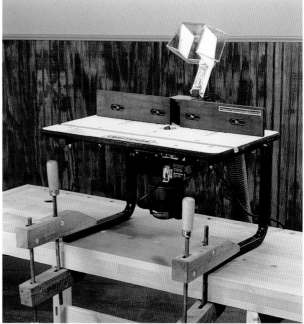

This commercial benchtop table has frame-style open base, flip-up blade guard, two-piece fence, vacuum port, and base-mounted switch. Always clamp the base to the supporting workbench for safest use.

Router Bits

Router bits are offered in many different styles and shapes and are made from either high-speed steel (HSS), solid carbide, or carbide-tipped steel. Carbide-tipped bits are by far the most common because they offer a good combination of durability and price. HSS bits are economy bits used with softer woods for short durations and then discarded. Solid carbide bits are expensive and limited to a few bit styles.

Knowing a little about the basic design elements of router bits will help you select the proper bits and give you points to compare when shopping.

BIT ANATOMY

All router bits have a shank, which is chucked into the router collet; a body; and cutters (although some bits have only one). The flutes are the cutaway spaces in front of the cutters. Flutes are sometimes called gullets or chip pockets because they provide a space for catching and ejecting the waste chips removed by the cutters. Bits that are piloted, or bearing-guided, have a ball-bearing pilot attached to the shank that controls the bit's cutting depth, although some pilots come in the form of a small, solid pin on the end of the bit or a smooth section of the shank that serves as the pilot.

The photo here shows the basic elements of a router bit and some of the terms commonly used for bit specification. Note that the "usable length" of the shank includes only the completely cylindrical portion. The area where the shank cuts away into the flute (or where it flares out as it meets the bit body) should not be placed into the collet and therefore doesn't count as usable length. This dimension typically is not provided by the manufacturer, so you'll have to measure it yourself when choosing a bit.

Overall diameter is an important consideration for several reasons. First, the bit must be smaller than the center hole in your router's subbase. If it's too big, you'll have to find or make an alternative subbase. Second, large-diameter bits are safer and more effective at slower speeds—as a general rule, bits over 1¼" in diameter should run at less than 18,000 rpm. You need a variable-speed router to use these bits properly. Bits over 1¾" in diameter are often tricky to use and typically should be used only on a router table.

Router bits are commonly available with ¼" and ½" shank diameters. As a general rule, ½" shanks are

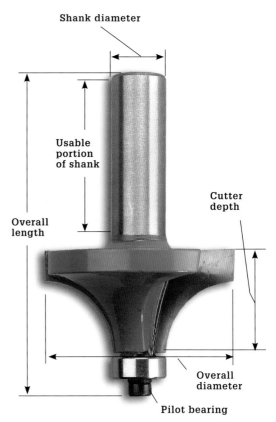

When purchasing router bits, you will see specifications including the diameter, shank size, and height or cutter depth. For some roundover bits, the radius of the rounded section also may be given.

Bits without bearings are designed for grooving a workpiece rather than forming an edge. Look for bits with a clean finish and a high-quality cutter. Carbide bits stay sharp longer than high-speed steel bits. Painted coatings reduce friction and provide greater visibility.

stiffer and stronger, making them more resistant to vibration, deflection, and breakage. Larger-diameter bits often cost the same as their ¼" counterparts.

A bit's cutting edges can reveal a lot about its quality, and they directly affect performance and longevity. Better bits are made with micrograin carbide, which wears slower and cuts cleaner than coarse-grade carbide. Check the grind of each cutter by running a fingernail along the front and back edges. They should be smooth and flat.

Many bits have painted or coated bodies. This smooth coating reduces friction and resin buildup, speeds waste ejection, and prevents corrosion. The coatings also improve the visibility of the cutter during use.

Although there is no official method for classifying the hundreds of different types of router bits, it is simple to group them by the type of work that they do, which in turn dictates certain design characteristics. For example, most grooving bits have plunge-cut capabilities, while edge-forming bits are usually piloted.

GROOVING BITS

The primary grooving tool, and perhaps the most versatile, is the straight bit. This has both side and bottom cutters, for cutting dadoes and rabbets and for trimming a workpiece. There is a great selection of decorative grooving bits to choose from, used for everything from cutting flutes to freehand carving. Some of the most popular are core-box, V-groove, veining, and point-cutting bits. These bits plunge vertically into the workpiece and then cut a decorative profile horizontally.

EDGE-FORMING BITS

Edge-forming bits cut decorative profiles into the edges of stock and into the faces of narrow trim material. Edge forming is probably the most common type of routing and involves the greatest variety of bit types. Most edge-forming bits are piloted, with an attached bearing that rolls along the workpiece, so that the bit cuts at a uniform depth. Bargain bits with solid nonbearing pilots have a tendency to burn or scar the workpiece and should be avoided. Most edge-forming bits have bearings at the end of the bit, and in some cases the bearing can be changed to alter the bit's cutting depth.

The decorative profiles on edge-forming bits allow you to cut everything from a simple roundover or chamfer to traditional details such as ogee, cavetto, cove, and bead. You can use any combination of edge-forming bits to mill your custom molding.

Some guided bits come with a variety of bearings of different sizes to change cutting depth.

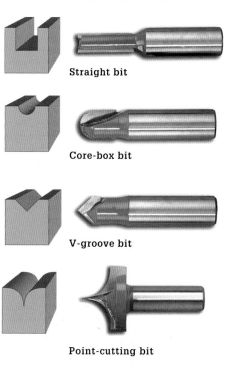

Straight bit

Core-box bit

V-groove bit

Point-cutting bit

EDGE-FORMING BITS

Roundover bit

Ogee bit with bead

Multi-form bit

Multibeading bit

Thin Moldings

Creating your own thin trim moldings is a simple process with the right tools. There are three different methods for creating your own thin trim moldings that utilize different types of cutter heads. The first method requires a tablesaw with a molding head. The second option uses a router with an edge-forming bit. The third option requires a shaper. A shaper is a machine dedicated to machining profiles into various types of stock. Shapers are generally expensive machines used only in production cabinet and millwork shops. For do-it-yourselfers, it makes the most sense to concentrate on the first two methods.

A molding head mounted in a table saw is a powerful tool for making larger quantities of profiled moldings. One great advantage to this setup versus a router table is that you can cut complex profiles in a single pass.

Using a tablesaw with a molding head is a fairly straightforward operation that produces excellent results with the proper setup. Molding heads consist of a center hub that accepts interchangeable cutters called knives. Knives come in many profiles for both conventional and unusual types of moldings. Molding heads are available from a variety of stores, either in kits with multiple knife profiles or as individual knife sets for a specific profile.

Exercise extreme caution when using a molding head. Kickback guards and splitters must be removed from the tablesaw, so safety is of even greater concern. Molding heads only have two to four knives that can be easily overwhelmed with too much material removal. Overloading a molding head leads to kickback.

With a multitude of router bit profiles to choose from, it's hard to beat a good midsize router for producing smaller moldings. In the example shown, router bits with bearing guides are mounted in a router table. This setup was chosen for speed, accuracy, and safety. Because the bits in this example have guide bearings, use of a router table is not necessary, but defects from the edge of your workpiece will be more visible when using a handheld router.

Always mill more stock than necessary to complete the job by 10 percent. Custom-milled moldings are difficult to recreate, and the extra material and time will pay off later if the piece is needed. Purchase material that is as close to the best grade available as possible. This will minimize scrap due to knots and other imperfections.

If you own a jointer and a tablesaw, you may want to purchase rough-sawn material and mill it yourself to save money. If you do not own these tools, you will have to purchase material that has already been planed to the proper thickness and has one straight edge, otherwise known as "straight-line ripped." It is important that the material you purchase be milled to precise dimensions.

If you're making narrow moldings, shape the profile along the edge of wider stock, and then rip the molding free with a standard blade. This keeps your hands a safer distance from the knives and makes it easier to control the cuts.

For those instances when you must shape the edge of narrow workpieces, make a shroud around the knives to hold workpieces as you feed them through the blade. Here's how (see photo and illustration below): Attach a sacrificial rip fence; then fasten another scrap with a flat edge to the wood fence to form a top hold-down. Position the top support on the wood fence so its height off the saw table matches the width of the workpieces you'll be milling. The top support thickness should match the workpiece thickness. Fasten a side support to the top support to act like a solid-surface featherboard alongside the cut. Make the top and side supports shorter than the length of the workpieces so the workpiece ends will protrude out from the shroud on both ends. This helps you maintain a better degree of control over the workpieces while feeding them into the knives.

To mill profiles with this blade shroud, set the knives to make shallow passes of ⅛" at a time. Feed workpieces into the shroud with a scrap of workpiece stock that fits into the shroud opening. Push the workpiece all the way through before shutting off the saw and removing the pushing scrap. If you're milling lots of strips with this setup, feed them end to end so the next workpiece serves as a push stick for the previous one.

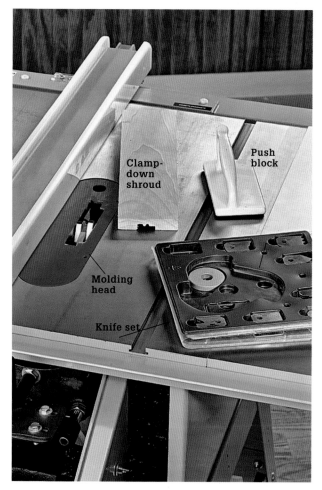

A molding head consists of a center hub that accepts sets of interchangeable molding cutters called knives.

How to Make a Fence Shroud for a Molding Head

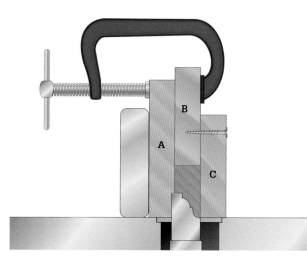

To cut molding profiles onto narrow strips, create a shroud of scrap pieces attached to the rip fence like this. The scrap closest to the rip fence (A) keeps the molding knives away from the metal rip fence. A second scrap over the knives (B) acts as a hold-down, and its thickness should match the workpiece thickness. A third scrap in front (C) keeps workpieces from drifting away from the rip fence during shaping. Feed strips one after the next so they act as push sticks.

Simple Base Molding

Base moldings and other moldings with profiled edges are perfect projects for making in your home workshop. You can produce them very efficiently by employing the following method. Start by choosing an edge-profiling bit that you like for the top profile, such as the ogee bit and the roundover bit shown below. Then, select wood stock that is a little more than twice the width of your planned molding height (for example, to make 5½"-tall molding, select 12" wide stock). Then, rout the edge profiles into both edges of the stock on a router table. Now all you need to do is rip the stock down the middle and you'll have two identical strips of molding.

Tools & Materials ▸

Router table with midsize router
Edge-profiling bit

Tablesaw
Prepared stock
Eye protection

Custom base molding is relatively easy to make. It can be simple and made from common lumber like the base molding seen here (you'll save a lot of money making it yourself) or it can have a unique profile and be made from any wood you choose, even an exotic wood.

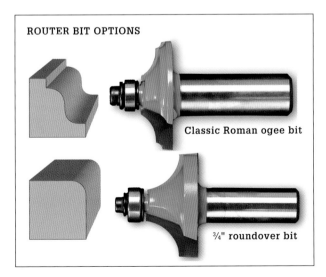

ROUTER BIT OPTIONS

Classic Roman ogee bit

¾" roundover bit

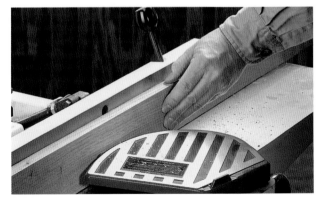

TIP: If you own a jointer, you may choose to joint both edges of the workpiece smooth before routing the subsequent profiles. For best results, alternate between the router, tablesaw, and jointer for smoother, cleaner edges.

How to Make Simple Base Moldings

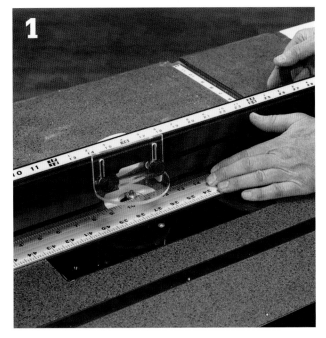

Prepare ¾" thick material to the maximum board width possible with two straightedges. Set the fence on the router table so that it is flush with the front edge of the bearing guide. Use a straightedge to help align the fence. If your stock is rough, set the fence slightly in front of the bearing guide so the fence guides the cut.

Use scrap material to fine-tune the height of the router bit. Adjust the height until you achieve the desired profile. Check the workpiece for troublesome tearout areas and determine optimum test-feed rates when running scrap material.

Rout the edges of your prepared material one side at a time, maintaining an even feed rate and applying adequate downward and lateral pressure to the workpiece. Profile both edges.

Set the tablesaw fence to rip the profiled molding stock in half, and then rip-cut the stock to release two sections of molding that have a profile on one edge and are square-cut on the other edge. Sand the square edge of the molding to remove rough saw blade marks.

Creating Custom Profiled Casing

Routing a profile across a 3"-wide piece of stock is a task usually left for a shaper with custom knives. But if you use a heavy-duty 1/2"a-collet router and an assortment of profiling bits, you can replicate just about any complex casing profile that a shaper can produce.

Tools & Materials ▸

Router table with
heavy-duty router
Prepared stock,
¾ × 3"

Router bits (chamfer,
vertical ogee,
handrail)

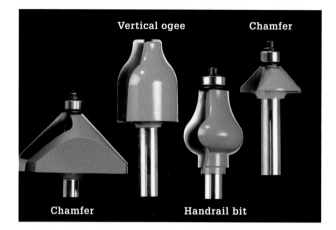

Bits you'll need typically include a chamfer, vertical ogee, and handrail bit.

Sophisticated casing profiles can be achieved by shaping the face of a board with an assortment of different profiling router bits. The casing seen here was created with chamfer bits (two sizes), a handrail bit and a vertical ogee bit.

How to Create Profiled Casing

Load a chamfer bit into your router and place the router in the router table. Adjust the height of the bit and the fence so that the workpiece is guided by the fence and and so that all but ⅟₁₆" of the edge is machined. Run the molding through the bit at an even rate to avoid burning the material.

Unplug the router and remove the chamfer bit. Load the vertical ogee bit into the router and place the router in the table. Adjust the height of the bit so that the bottom edge of the cutter lines up with the chamfered edge from the first pass, maintaining a casing thickness of approximately ¼".

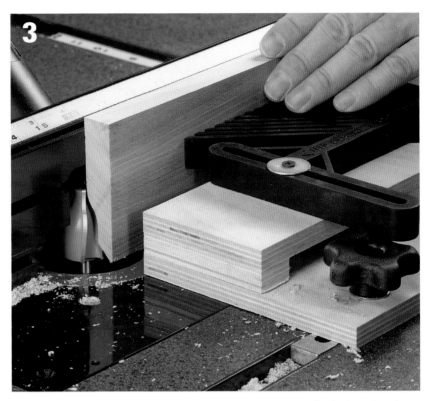

Run the molding through the vertical ogee bit using elevated featherboards to keep the workpiece tight against the fence. If necessary, make multiple shallow passes to avoid overloading the router and to extend the life of the bit.

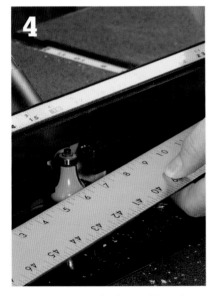

Remove the vertical ogee bit and replace it with the handrail bit. Use a straightedge to align the fence with the bit bearing. Raise the bit to its full height and run a piece of scrap material to check the cut, using multiple shallow passes if necessary. Note: Multiple shallow passes require moving the fence further in front of the bearing.

Run the material through the handrail bit at a slow, steady rate. Use featherboards and push sticks as necessary. After the final pass, lightly sand each work piece with fine-grit sandpaper.

Chair Rail

Creating your own custom chair rail is a great opportunity for the novice woodworker or carpenter to become better acquainted with table routing and the capabilities of a midsized router. Because chair rails vary in dimension and style so dramatically from one house to the next, your options when designing one are endless. Chair rails basically fall between 1½" and 5" wide and range in depth from ½" to 1½".

To make the chair rail shown, four passes are required with the router. Two passes are done with an edge-forming bit, and two use the router fence as a guide. The result is a symmetrical chair rail that is neither boring nor overly elaborate.

When choosing router bits for your chair rail, take into account the style of the door and window casings in the room. Chair rails that have a greater depth than the outer edge of the casings require returns to avoid ugly joints. These returns can be difficult to cut and may complicate your installation.

Tools & Materials ▸

Midsized router	Router table
Edge-forming bits	Prepared stock
Grooving bits	Eye protection

Most stock chair rail profiles are rather ornate and curvilinear. If your tastes run more toward the beefy and geometric, making your own molding is a good way to get the trim you want.

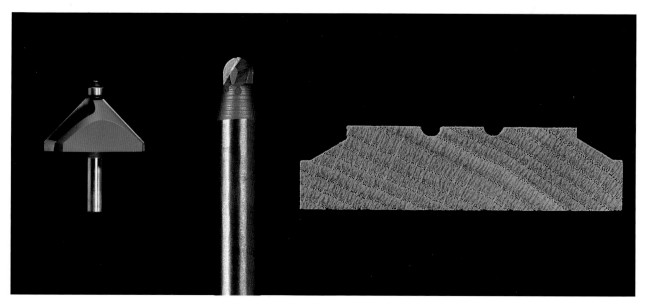

The chair rail molding seen here is made from 1 x 4 red oak stock. The chamfered edges are made with a piloted chamfer bit (left). The fluting is done with a grooving bit, also called a beading bit (middle).

How to Make Chair Rail Molding

Load the grooving bit in the router and set up the router in a table. Set the fence of the router table so that the grooves will fall ¼" from the center. Adjust the height of the grooving bit so that the width of the groove will be about ⅛" wide.

With the bit in the proper position, run the prepared stock through the bit. Make a pass on each edge of the workpieces, creating symmetrical lines off the center. Run the stock at a uniform rate, keeping it flat on the table.

Remove the grooving bit and replace it with the edge-forming bit. Remove the fence assembly from the table and install a starting pin or fulcrum point. Test the height of the bit by running scrap material, adjusting the height of the bit as desired.

With the bit at the desired height, run the prepared stock, making a pass on both edges. For assymmetrical work, change the bit after making a pass on one edge only, and replace it with a different style of edge-forming bit with similar dimensions.

Cove Molding on a Tablesaw

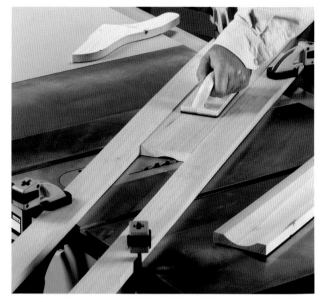

ove molding is similar to crown molding, but with simpler edge profiles. Most lumberyards will carry a couple of cove options, but for different sizes or wood species, or simply to save money, you can use your tablesaw to make a lateral scoop cut that converts flat 1x stock into cove stock. If you're installing it as crown, you'll need to make relief cuts on the edges so it has flat surfaces to fit against the wall and the ceiling.

Moving your workpiece across the tablesaw blade from the side is tricky and can be dangerous if you do not have the correct jig and a fair amount of experience with your tablesaw. The jig is essentially a parallelogram with hinged ends. The jig used here is shop-built, but you can find them for sale from woodworking supply retailers.

As with all operations on a tablesaw, use caution when cutting coves. Attempting to remove too much material at one time may result in kickback of your material, or cause damage to the arbor of your tablesaw. Always use appropriate safety gear, including push pads and a push stick. As you push the material through the blade, maintain constant downward pressure on the workpiece. Try to sustain a uniform feed rate of the material, slowing your rate if the blade becomes bogged down.

Cove molding has a lateral scoop cut that can be made on any dimensional stock using a tablesaw or a shaper. To make the cut with a tablesaw, the workpiece is fed across the spinning saw blade from the side. A jig is necessary for setting up the cut.

Tools & Materials ▸

Tablesaw with cross-cut blade	Carriage bolts
Clamps	Washers
T-bevel	Wing nuts
Straight dimensional lumber	Prepared material (for cove molding)
	Eye protection

Cove Jigs ▸

A factory-made cove-cutting jig is used to create a path for your workpiece. These tools usually key off the miter gauge slots in your saw table. An alternative is to build your own jig. The one seen in the sequence on the next page is used to set up cuts. Straightedge guides are clamped to the saw table to provide actual cutting guidance.

You can build an adjustable parallelogram jig like it using straight strips of 2"-wide scrap. Make the long sides 4 ft. and the short ends 1 ft. Attach the parts with short carriage bolts, washers, and wing nuts so you can adjust the jig shape by hand. The jig will establish the angle you'll need to cut a cove with a specific curvature and width. If you choose to use your own jig with straightedge guides, it is a good idea to do a test run through the "tunnel" with the blade completely lowered beneath the tabletop and the saw turned off. This will ensure that the workpiece fits snugly between the straightedges. It also ensures that the workpiece will not bind up halfway through a cut due to warping of the piece.

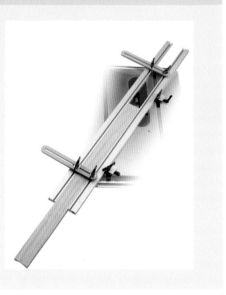

How to Cut Coves with a Tablesaw

Unplug your tablesaw. Then, mark the scoop profile on the end of a workpiece and use it as a gauge. Raise the tablesaw blade to full cutting height. **Note:** This is for setting up purposes; the actual cut must be made in several passes.

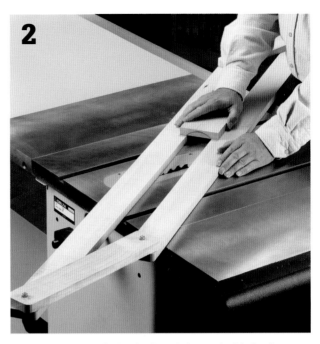

Establish the angle for the jig, relative to the blade. The closer the jig is to perpendicular to the blade, the steeper the scoop will be. Adjust the jig arms so the ends of the scoop fall as close as possible to your profile marks.

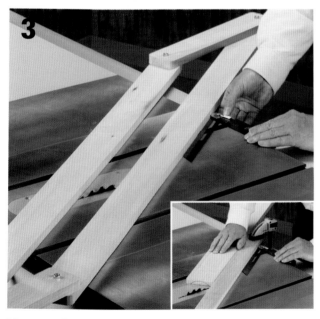

Measure the angle of the jig arms relative to the saw table. Then remove the jig and replace it with a pair of long straightedge guides. Use a workpiece and a T-bevel set to the correct angle as guides for positioning the straightedges (inset). Clamp the straightedge to the saw table, keeping the path between them clear.

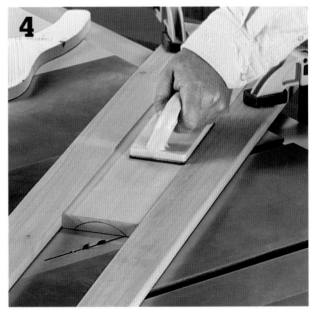

Fit the workpiece between the straightedges and test to make sure it slides freely without binding. Lower the saw blade to ¼" cutting depth. With the workpiece clear, turn on your tablesaw. Feed the workpiece through using a hold-down and a push stick. Turn off the saw, raise the blade slightly, and repeat the cut. Continue making slightly deeper cuts until the full depth is reached. If you are making more than one piece of cove molding, cut all the workpieces at each cutting depth before raising the blade. Bevel-rip the edges if desired.

Metric Conversions

English to Metric

To Convert:	To:	Multiply by:
Inches	Millimeters	25.4
Inches	Centimeters	2.54
Feet	Meters	0.305
Yards	Meters	0.914
Square inches	Square centimeters	6.45
Square feet	Square meters	0.093
Square yards	Square meters	0.836
Ounces	Milliliters	30.0
Pints (U.S.)	Liters	0.473 (Imp. 0.568)
Quarts (U.S.)	Liters	0.946 (Imp. 1.136)
Gallons (U.S.)	Liters	3.785 (Imp. 4.546)
Ounces	Grams	28.4
Pounds	Kilograms	0.454

To Convert:	To:	Multiply by:
Millimeters	Inches	0.039
Centimeters	Inches	0.394
Meters	Feet	3.28
Meters	Yards	1.09
Square centimeters	Square inches	0.155
Square meters	Square feet	10.8
Square meters	Square yards	1.2
Milliliters	Ounces	.033
Liters	Pints (U.S.)	2.114 (Imp. 1.76)
Liters	Quarts (U.S.)	1.057 (Imp. 0.88)
Liters	Gallons (U.S.)	0.264 (Imp. 0.22)
Grams	Ounces	0.035
Kilograms	Pounds	2.2

Converting Temperatures

Convert degrees Fahrenheit (F) to degrees Celsius (C) by following this simple formula: Subtract 32 from the Fahrenheit temperature reading. Then multiply that number by $5/9$. For example, $77°F - 32 = 45$. $45 \times 5/9 = 25°C$.

To convert degrees Celsius to degrees Fahrenheit, multiply the Celsius temperature reading by $9/5$. Then, add 32. For example, $25°C \times 9/5 = 45$. $45 + 32 = 77°F$.

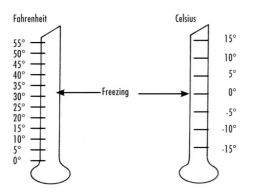

Metric Plywood Panels

Metric plywood panels are commonly available in two sizes: 1,200 mm × 2,400 mm and 1,220 mm × 2,400 mm, which is roughly equivalent to a 4 × 8-ft. sheet. Standard and Select sheathing panels come in standard thicknesses, while Sanded grade panels are available in special thicknesses.

Standard Sheathing Grade		Sanded Grade	
7.5 mm	(⁵/₁₆ in.)	6 mm	(⁴/₁₇ in.)
9.5 mm	(³/₈ in.)	8 mm	(⁵/₁₆ in.)
12.5 mm	(½ in.)	11 mm	(⁷/₁₆ in.)
15.5 mm	(⁵/₈ in.)	14 mm	(⁹/₁₆ in.)
18.5 mm	(¾ in.)	17 mm	(²/₃ in.)
20.5 mm	(¹³/₁₆ in.)	19 mm	(¾ in.)
22.5 mm	(⁷/₈ in.)	21 mm	(¹³/₁₆ in.)
25.5 mm	(1 in.)	24 mm	(¹⁵/₁₆ in.)

Lumber Dimensions

Nominal - U.S.	Actual - U.S. (in inches)	Metric
1 × 2	¾ × 1½	19 × 38 mm
1 × 3	¾ × 2½	19 × 64 mm
1 × 4	¾ × 3½	19 × 89 mm
1 × 5	¾ × 4½	19 × 114 mm
1 × 6	¾ × 5½	19 × 140 mm
1 × 7	¾ × 6¼	19 × 159 mm
1 × 8	¾ × 7¼	19 × 184 mm
1 × 10	¾ × 9¼	19 × 235 mm
1 × 12	¾ × 11¼	19 × 286 mm
1¼ × 4	1 × 3½	25 × 89 mm
1¼ × 6	1 × 5½	25 × 140 mm
1¼ × 8	1 × 7¼	25 × 184 mm
1¼ × 10	1 × 9¼	25 × 235 mm
1¼ × 12	1 × 11¼	25 × 286 mm
1½ × 4	1¼ × 3½	32 × 89 mm
1½ × 6	1¼ × 5½	32 × 140 mm
1½ × 8	1¼ × 7¼	32 × 184 mm
1½ × 10	1¼ × 9¼	32 × 235 mm
1½ × 12	1¼ × 11¼	32 × 286 mm
2 × 4	1½ × 3½	38 × 89 mm
2 × 6	1½ × 5½	38 × 140 mm
2 × 8	1½ × 7¼	38 × 184 mm
2 × 10	1½ × 9¼	38 × 235 mm
2 × 12	1½ × 11¼	38 × 286 mm
3 × 6	2½ × 5½	64 × 140 mm
4 × 4	3½ × 3½	89 × 89 mm
4 × 6	3½ × 5½	89 × 140 mm

Liquid Measurement Equivalents

1 Pint	= 16 Fluid Ounces	= 2 Cups
1 Quart	= 32 Fluid Ounces	= 2 Pints
1 Gallon	= 128 Fluid Ounces	= 4 Quarts

Counterbore, Shank & Pilot Hole Diameters

Screw Size	Counterbore Diameter for Screw Head (in inches)	Clearance Hole for Screw Shank (in inches)	Pilot Hole Diameter	
			Hard Wood (in inches)	Soft Wood (in inches)
#1	.146 ($\frac{9}{64}$)	$\frac{5}{64}$	$\frac{3}{64}$	$\frac{1}{32}$
#2	$\frac{1}{4}$	$\frac{3}{32}$	$\frac{3}{64}$	$\frac{1}{32}$
#3	$\frac{1}{4}$	$\frac{7}{64}$	$\frac{1}{16}$	$\frac{3}{64}$
#4	$\frac{1}{4}$	$\frac{1}{8}$	$\frac{1}{16}$	$\frac{3}{64}$
#5	$\frac{1}{4}$	$\frac{1}{8}$	$\frac{5}{64}$	$\frac{1}{16}$
#6	$\frac{5}{16}$	$\frac{9}{64}$	$\frac{3}{32}$	$\frac{5}{64}$
#7	$\frac{5}{16}$	$\frac{5}{32}$	$\frac{3}{32}$	$\frac{5}{64}$
#8	$\frac{3}{8}$	$\frac{11}{64}$	$\frac{1}{8}$	$\frac{3}{32}$
#9	$\frac{3}{8}$	$\frac{11}{64}$	$\frac{1}{8}$	$\frac{3}{32}$
#10	$\frac{3}{8}$	$\frac{3}{16}$	$\frac{1}{8}$	$\frac{7}{64}$
#11	$\frac{1}{2}$	$\frac{3}{16}$	$\frac{5}{32}$	$\frac{9}{64}$
#12	$\frac{1}{2}$	$\frac{7}{32}$	$\frac{9}{64}$	$\frac{1}{8}$

Nails

Nail lengths are identified by numbers from 4 to 60 followed by the letter "d," which stands for "penny." For general framing and repair work, use common or box nails. Common nails are best suited to framing work where strength is important. Box nails are smaller in diameter than common nails, which makes them easier to drive and less likely to split wood. Use box nails for light work and thin materials. Most common and box nails have a cement or vinyl coating that improves their holding power.

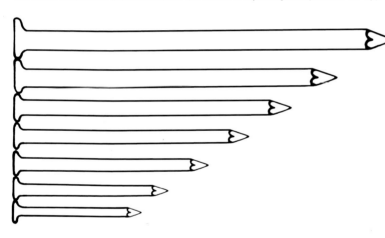

lbs.	mm	in.
20d	102 mm	4"
16d	89 mm	3½"
10d	76 mm	3"
8d	64 mm	2½"
6d	51 mm	2"
5d	44 mm	1¾"
4d	38 mm	1½"

Resources/Credits

Power Tools & Accessories
Black & Decker Corp.
800-544-6986
www.blackanddecker.com

Work boots and shoes
Red Wing Shoes Co.
800-733-9464
www.redwingshoes.com

Spring miter clamps (Featured in DVD)
Collins Tool Co.
888-838-8988
www.collinstool.com

General information on wood trim
Moulding & Millwork Producers Association (MMPA)
800-550-7889
www.wmmpa.com

Nonwood trim & millwork
Fypon, LTD
800-446-9373
www.fypon.com

Index

CREATIVE PUBLISHING international

NOTE TO READERS

The DVD disk included with this book is offered as a free premium to buyers of this book.

The live video demonstrations are designed to be viewed on electronic devices suitable for viewing standard DVD video discs, including most television DVD players, as well as a Mac or PC computer equipped with a DVD-compatible disc drive and standard multi-media software.

In addition, your DVD-compatible computer will allow you to read the electronic version of the book. The electronic version is provided in a standard PDF form, which is readable by any software compatible with that format, including Adobe Reader.

To access the electronic pages, open the directory of your computer's DVD drive, and click on the icon with the image of this book cover.

The electronic book carries the same copyright restrictions as the print version. You are welcome to use it in any way that is useful for you, including printing the pages for your own use. You can also loan the disc to friends or family members, much the way you would loan a printed book.

However, we do request that you respect copyright law and the integrity of this book by not attempting to make electronic copies of this disc, or by distributing the files electronically via the internet.

Creative Publishing
international

400 First Avenue North • Suite 300 • Minneapolis, MN 55401 • 800-328-0590, opt 2 • www.creativepub.c